Recent Researches in the Music of the Baroque Era, 134

Domenico Allegri

Music for an Academic Defense (Rome, 1617)

Edited by Antony John
with Historical and Textual Commentary
by Louise Rice and Clare Woods

A-R Editions, Inc.
Middleton, Wisconsin

Performance parts are available from the publisher.

A-R Editions, Inc., Middleton, Wisconsin 53562
© 2004 by A-R Editions, Inc.

All rights reserved. No part of this book may be reproduced or transmitted in any form by any electronic or mechanical means (including photocopying, recording, or information storage and retrieval) without permission in writing from the publisher.

The purchase of this edition does not convey the right to perform it in public, nor to make a recording of it for any purpose. Such permission must be obtained in advance from the publisher.

A-R Editions is pleased to support scholars and performers in their use of *Recent Researches* material for study or performance. Subscribers to any of the *Recent Researches* series, as well as patrons of subscribing institutions, are invited to apply for information about our "Copyright Sharing Policy."

Printed in the United States of America

ISBN 0-89579-552-3
ISSN 0484-0828

♾ The paper used in this publication meets the minimum requirements of the American National Standard for Information Sciences—Permanence of Paper for Printed Library Materials, ANSI Z39.48-1984.

Contents

Acknowledgments   vi

Introduction   vii

  The Philosophy Defense of Ilario Frumenti, *Louise Rice*   vii
    The Festive Academic Defense in Seicento Rome   vii
    Frumenti's Defense and Its Medicean Program   ix
    Allegri's *Modi* and Roman Defense Music   xiv
  Poetry into Song: Lyrics for a Thesis Defense, *Clare Woods*   xvii
  Performance Practice, *Antony John*   xviii
  Appendix   xix
  Notes   xx

Texts and Translations   xxiv

Plates   xxv

Music for an Academic Defense

  Sol   3
  Saturnus   26
  Mercurius   43

Critical Report   55

  Source   55
  Editorial Methods   55
  Critical Notes   56
  Notes   57

Acknowledgments

This edition represents a collaborative undertaking, in the most positive sense, between scholars in different disciplines. Louise Rice, an art historian who came across the music while researching seventeenth-century Roman thesis prints, sets the work in its historical context and reunites it with the graphic material that originally accompanied it; Clare Woods, a Latinist, provides an analysis of the text; and Antony John, the volume's editor, is responsible for all matters musical. We owe a special debt of gratitude to Alexander Silbiger, our uncredited collaborator, whose mentoring of the project has been at all times inspirational. Of the many others who lent their support at various stages, particular thanks to Michael Dodds, who gamely assumed the role of Roman correspondent, and Stephanie Vial and the Duke University Collegium Musicum, who presented the first modern performance of this work under the direction of Antony John in November 2000. In addition, Louise Rice wishes personally to thank Giuseppe Gerbino, Frederick Hammond, T. Frank Kennedy S. J., Noel O'Regan, John Rice, and Stewart Smith. Finally, a hearty thanks to the editors at A-R Editions whose perseverance and professionalism have improved each and every page of this volume.

Introduction

The Philosophy Defense of Ilario Frumenti, by Louise Rice

In 1617, Ilario Frumenti, a young nobleman from Como, defended philosophical theses in the great hall of the Jesuits' Roman College (fig. 1). It was a festive occasion, and although no description has come down to us, the printed materials produced in connection with it attest to the pageantry that surrounded the event. These printed materials include the elaborate allegorical engraving that adorned the student's thesis broadsheet; the Latin odes written by one of his Jesuit professors, Cesare Laurenti, and published in the form of a slim libretto; and the musical setting of three of the odes, composed by Domenico Allegri for two choirs with soloists and instrumental accompaniment and published in a separate but matching booklet. It is the existence of the last of these items, the printed score, that earns Frumenti's defense a place of special importance in the history of Roman music. Choral singing was a regular feature of public academic defenses throughout the seicento, but because the music was occasional (that is, commissioned for a specific occasion and meant to be performed only once), it was not normally printed, nor was any effort made to preserve it in manuscript form once it had served its purpose, with the result that almost none of it survives. Frumenti's defense was unusual and possibly unique among the thousands of defenses that took place in Rome in the seventeenth century in that the music written to accompany it was printed at the time of the event. Other specimens of defense music may yet come to light, in either printed or manuscript form, but for the moment Allegri's score for the 1617 defense of Ilario Frumenti is the only known example of what was a major category of Roman musical production throughout the period from the late sixteenth century to the mid-eighteenth century. The score is thus of exceptional interest not only as a work of considerable merit in its own right and one of the few surviving compositions by Domenico Allegri, but as a window onto a much larger musical phenomenon.

The Festive Academic Defense in Seicento Rome

Unlike academic defenses today, low-key affairs usually conducted behind closed doors, the baroque defense was a form of public spectacle, attracting large and aristocratic audiences who attended not only to witness the performance of the student but to enjoy the festive trappings that accompanied it. In Rome it was not unusual for half a dozen cardinals to be present at the defense of a particularly talented or well-connected student, and in exceptional instances the whole college of cardinals turned out, along with scores of prelates, princes, ambassadors, noblemen, and dignitaries from every walk of life. When the son of the Spanish ambassador defended philosophical theses at the Roman College in 1602, every cardinal in Rome was present, along with all of the prelates at the papal court.[1] Twenty-four cardinals and 90 prelates attended the philosophy defense of Francisco de Guevara, son of the duke of Bovino, at the Roman College in 1614;[2] and at the defense in 1676 of Benedetto Pamphili the audience included 41 cardinals and 160 prelates, along with literally thousands of others.[3] Such was the crush on occasions like these that Swiss guards were often employed to assist in crowd control. The size and the quality of the audiences they attracted bear witness to the importance of thesis defenses in the cultural life of the baroque city.

The defendant typically dedicated his theses to a cardinal or prince—someone with money and influence who could potentially assist him in his future career. The dedicatee was a key figure at the defense. He lent dignity to the occasion by attending it, and in return he was celebrated in encomiastic speeches delivered by the student at the start and at the end of the defense, as well as in the artistic program that accompanied it throughout.

What exactly went on at an academic defense? The main event was a disputation, that is, a formal oral examination during which the student presented a series of theses, or conclusions as they were generally called, that he elaborated in response to challenges posed by his examiners. The conclusions were philosophical, theological, legal, or medical in content, depending on the candidate's course of studies. Frumenti, for example, had completed the three-year course in philosophy and defended philosophical theses. The disputation, a product of the medieval university, had by the seventeenth century evolved into a highly rehearsed and stylized exercise designed to give the student an opportunity to show off his logical and rhetorical skills. A defendant did well if he held his own against his examiners, spoke eloquently and persuasively on a variety of topics, cited classical and scholastic sources in support of his theses, and in general handled himself with ease and grace. Since only the brightest and most accomplished students

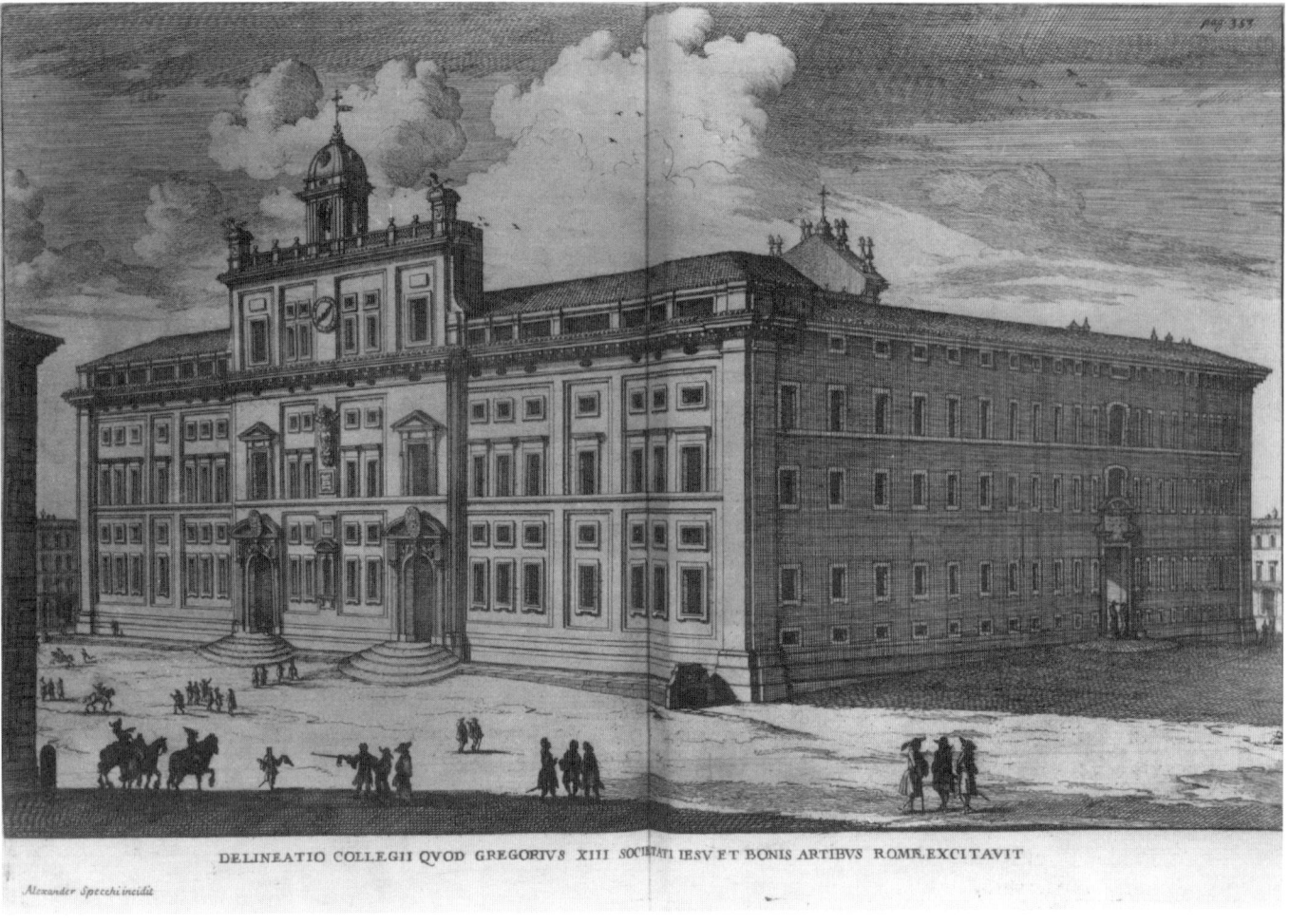

Figure 1. Alessandro Specchi, View of the Roman College. Courtesy of the Bibliotheca Hertziana, Rome.

were allowed the privilege of undergoing a public defense, the quality of the performance was generally high.

The disputation at the heart of the defense was set within a framework of art, poetry, and music designed to enhance the audience's enjoyment and, in particular, to gratify and delight the dedicatee. A broadsheet listing the student's conclusions was distributed to the members of the audience at the outset of the defense. It usually featured an engraving, or thesis print, which provided a visual counterpart to the dedicatory text that accompanied it. Students spared no expense in their effort to make their broadsheets as gorgeous as possible: those who could afford to do so issued, in addition to the copies printed on paper, a deluxe limited edition printed on colored silk, trimmed in gold lace, and embroidered with personal devices, which they handed out to the more important members of the audience. One or more poems, written specifically for the occasion by one of the professors at the student's institution, accompanied the broadsheet. Published in a separate libretto and distributed to the audience at the same time as the broadsheet, the poems were also set to music and sung at key moments during the defense. The thesis print and the poems were intricately related. They often involved a common heraldic conceit, alluding to the coat of arms of the dedicatee and melding visual and verbal imagery in highly inventive ways. The audience experienced the thesis print, the poetry, and the music simultaneously. As they unfolded the broadsheet and were confronted for the first time with its dense and complex imagery, they were hearing the choirs singing Latin verses that provided an explanatory key to understanding the picture. Conversely, as they followed the sung text, with its intricate rhetorical figures, they saw its allegorical language given concrete visual articulation in the thesis print. The defense was thus a multimedia entertainment combining visual, literary, and musical elements within its carefully orchestrated programmatic structure.[4]

The event took place either in the main hall of the student's institution (as in Frumenti's case) or in an affiliated church. The space was splendidly adorned for the occasion. Tapestries, damasks, and garlands of laurel were suspended from the walls; sweet-smelling petals or leaves carpeted the floor. At one end of the room stood a pulpit, from which the student addressed his audience. Rows of chairs and benches were arranged in front and on either side of the pulpit. Seating was strictly hierarchical. The dedicatee with his friends and associates and any other cardinals who were present sat in comfortable armchairs at the front, while others of lesser distinction were relegated to the hard benches near the back of the room. When the defense took place in the college hall, temporary *palchi* (risers) were erected on either side of the room for the singers and instrumentalists; when it took place in a church, the musicians generally performed from the permanent *coretti* (musicians' balconies) positioned symmetrically on either side of the nave.

Music was woven into the pageantry of the defense from beginning to end. Instrumental fanfares signaled the start of the event. Once the audience was seated, the first choral interlude was performed while the thesis broadsheets and librettos were distributed. The student then ascended the pulpit and delivered an introductory speech in praise of the dedicatee, after which the choirs sang a second time. At this point, the defense itself got underway, that is to say, the oral examination of the theses, during which the student responded to a series of arguments raised by his examiners. This in turn was followed by a third choral interlude, the student's closing speech in which he formally thanked his dedicatee and the audience as a whole for their attendance, and a brief but jubilant choral finale. Naturally, there was a certain amount of variation (sometimes there were three, sometimes four main sections of choral music; sometimes the broadsheets and librettos were handed out at the beginning, sometimes halfway through or at the end), but the basic pattern of the defense remained fairly constant from the late sixteenth through the middle of the eighteenth century. At a defense at the German College in 1592, for example, "there was singing at four points: at the beginning, after the preface, after the disputation, and after the thanksgiving."[5] Three-quarters of a century later, at the law defense of Giovanni Angelo Altemps at the Sapienza in 1666, music was incorporated in much the same way:

> The cardinals and Signor Prince Agostino Chigi entered the hall two by two in order of age. The musicians immediately began the symphony of instruments and the melody of voices, singing the first ode . . . , and the music continued while two gentlemen of the Altemps household on either side of the room courteously and discreetly distributed bunches of flowers to the cardinals, prelates, and others. . . . When the singing was finished, [the defendant] opened his performance with a prefatory address, most erudite and well-crafted, after which he went on to explain a text of canon law. . . . At that point the musicians performed the second ode, while at the same time the thesis broadsheets were distributed. . . . Once the distribution was completed, [the disputation took place]. . . . The disputation finished, the choir of musicians sang the third and final ode, while at the same time the librettos containing the texts that were sung . . . were handed out.[6]

Defense music was almost always polychoral, in keeping with the prevailing Roman fashion.[7] A defense that took place at the Roman College in 1592 was clearly unusual in having "good music, but without organ or other instruments, and with only one choir."[8] Two choirs were the norm, but we hear of performances involving four,[9] six,[10] or in exceptional cases as many as eight choirs. At a defense at the Roman College in 1654, "there was music performed by eight choirs of the choicest voices in Rome; and in addition there were two ensembles of instrumentalists, including four trumpets that accompanied the organ, a rare combination. Two of the trumpets played from the upper windows into the room."[11] A piece written for eight choirs required a minimum of thirty-two singers (assuming one voice per part and four parts per choir) plus instrumentalists, a very considerable force. No college with the possible exception of the German College had sufficient strength in house to undertake such performances, and the hiring of outside singers, despite occasional strictures against it, was in fact common practice. The scale of defense music tended to grow as the century progressed, and by 1700 it was not unheard of for the singers to be accompanied by huge orchestras of sixty or more instrumentalists.[12] Frumenti's defense, which took place nearer the beginning of the century, was a simpler affair from the musical standpoint and may have involved as few as a dozen performers altogether (eight singers and four instrumentalists).

Frumenti's Defense and Its Medicean Program

Almost nothing is known about our student, Ilario Frumenti, other than that he came from Como, was a member of the Parthenian Academy (an elite student sodality at the Roman College), and defended in philosophy in 1617. Since students typically completed the course in philosophy when they were in their early twenties, he was probably born around 1595. This would make him an exact contemporary of the man to whom he dedicated his conclusions, Cardinal Carlo de' Medici (1595–1666).

About the dedicatee we know a good deal more. The brother of Cosimo II, grand duke of Tuscany, Cardinal Carlo de' Medici represented Florentine interests at the papal court for half a century (fig. 2). He was known for his love of luxury and was an avid collector who filled his residences in Florence and Rome with superb works of art.[13] Carlo was elevated to the cardinalate in 1615 at the age of twenty and moved to Rome a few months later in April 1616. He was thus a relative newcomer both to the college of cardinals and to the city of Rome when he attended Frumenti's defense in 1617. How he came to sponsor Frumenti is uncertain. Ordinarily, students who dedicated their theses to Cardinal de' Medici were from his native Tuscany;[14] whereas Frumenti, a Lombard, had no regional claim to his patronage. There was, however, at least a tenuous connection between his family and the cardinal's, as Frumenti goes to some pains to spell out in the dedicatory preface to the poems published in connection with his defense. It stemmed from the fact that the Frumenti were joined by marriage to another noble family from Como, the Giovio, who were in turn allied to the Medici through the person of their most famous forebear, Paolo Giovio (1483–1552), the celebrated humanist historian and courtier to the Medici popes Leo X and Clement VII. Paolo Giovio had so ingratiated himself with the Medici that he was granted the exceptional privilege of quartering his family arms with theirs.[15] Thus young Frumenti claimed a chain of association linking his own family to the Giovio,

Figure 2. Anonymous, Cardinal Carlo de' Medici, ca. 1616. Galleria degli Uffizi, Florence.

Figure 3. Attributed to Matthaeus Greuter, Coats of Arms of the Giovio and Frumenti Families, in [Cesare Laurenti], *Illustrissimo Principi Carolo Medici . . . Caelestium Orbium Armoniam dicat Hilarius Frumentius . . .* (Rome, 1617). Courtesy of the Biblioteca Casanatense, Rome.

the Giovio to the Medici, and by extension Cardinal Carlo to himself. The conceit is given visual reiteration in an engraved plate at the end of the libretto, which features two escutcheons, on the right that of the Frumenti and that of the Giovio (incorporating the six *palle* [balls] of the Medici coat of arms) on the left, with the following explanatory caption: "With little pomp but great reverence, Ilario Frumenti of Como presents to Cardinal Carlo de' Medici the families Giovio and Frumenti, joined by blood, the one long since linked to the Medici name, the other but recently allied" (fig. 3).

In the preface to the poems Frumenti vows to follow in Paolo Giovio's footsteps in celebrating the Medici name. He thus sets the stage for the artistic program of his defense, which amounts to an elaborate and layered panegyric in praise of Cardinal de' Medici, expressed in image, verse, and song. Let us look first at the individual pieces of printed material that have come down to us, and then consider how they are interconnected.

Of Frumenti's thesis broadsheet, all that survives is the engraving (fig. 4).[16] Designed and executed by Matthaeus Greuter (ca. 1566–1638), it features the cardinal's heraldry as its principal theme. The six *palle* that form the Medici coat of arms are supported amid a glory of light by the planetary deities—Saturn, Mars, Mercury, Diana the Moon, Apollo the Sun with Venus at his side, and Jupiter (clockwise from the top)—with Eternity holding the cardinal's hat in position over the whole. The divinities, seated in chariots marked with the zodiacal symbols associated with them, hold their eponymous orbs in the order of their planetary distance from Earth, according to the Ptolemaic model. Thus the Moon is at the bottom and Saturn, the most distant of the planets known at that time, is at the top, while the others including the Sun are positioned in between. That Venus is depicted sharing Apollo's chariot is not merely a clever bit of poetic conflation designed to reconcile the seven celestial bodies with the six *palle* of the Medici coat of arms. It is also intended as an allusion to the critically important discovery made in 1610 that Venus, like the Moon, exhibits phases. Looking through his newly perfected telescope, the Florentine astronomer Galileo Galilei observed the waxing and waning of the planet and used the data he collected to demonstrate conclusively that Venus orbits the Sun. For Galileo this was proof that Copernicus was right and that the Sun rather than Earth was at the center of the universe. But others, including the Jesuit astronomers at the Roman College, took a more conservative view and, while accepting that Venus revolves around the Sun, nevertheless maintained that

Figure 4. Matthaeus Greuter, The Medici Arms Supported by the Celestial Bodies, thesis print of Ilario Frumenti, who defended in philosophy at the Roman College in 1617. Courtesy of the Bibliothèque nationale de France, Paris.

the Sun revolves around the Earth. By placing Venus in Apollo's chariot, Greuter affirms the modified Ptolemaic cosmology taught by the Jesuits while at the same time uses Galileo's discovery of the phases of Venus to craft a celestial compliment in honor of the dedicatee.[17]

In the sublunary landscape below, the river Arno, in a shell-shaped chariot pulled by Florentine lions, and Ceres, the goddess of agriculture, in a chariot pulled by dragons, approach one another from opposite corners. He holds three *palle* in reference to the dedicatee; she wears a wheat wreath and in her left hand holds three ears of wheat in reference to the student (Frumenti derives from *frumento*, meaning wheat or grain) and to his canting coat of arms, which includes among its elements three ears of wheat (fig. 3). Behind Ceres, Fortune, her forelock floating free, adds fleurs-de-lis to the uppermost *palla* of the Medici arms, alluding to the family's close ties to the crown of France. In the distance is a panoramic view of Florence, the cardinal's native city, with the principal Medicean landmarks clearly visible: the church of S. Lorenzo, Palazzo Vecchio with the Neptune fountain and the equestrian statue of Cosimo I, the Uffizi, Ponte Vecchio, and, just to the left of the dragon's wing, the Pitti Palace, the principal residence of the Medici in the seventeenth century.

Although Greuter's engraving is all that we have of Frumenti's broadsheet, it is not difficult to picture what the thing would have looked like intact. Publications of this kind tended to follow a standard formula. Accordingly, the print would have appeared at the top of the sheet; below it would have been a dedicatory inscription addressed to Cardinal de' Medici, expounding in elegant and ornate Latin on the themes developed in the image; and below the dedication, in the lower half of the sheet, would have been the conclusions themselves, arranged in two or three columns. The name of the printer and the time and place of the defense would have been indicated at the bottom of the page. Frumenti's broadsheet would have closely resembled, for example, the broadsheet of Fra Giovanni Dalla Torre, a Dominican friar who studied at the college attached to S. Maria sopra Minerva and defended theological theses there in 1634 (fig. 5). It was common practice for students of modest means to economize by reusing an existing thesis print. Dalla Torre reused the print originally commissioned by Frumenti, and although he introduced certain changes to the design

Figure 5. Thesis broadsheet of Fra Giovanni Dalla Torre, who defended in theology at the Dominican college of S. Maria sopra Minerva in 1634. Courtesy of the Collegio S. Isidoro, Rome.

Figure 6. Matthaeus Greuter, title page in [Cesare Laurenti], *Illustrissimo Principi Carolo Medici . . . Caelestium Orbium Armoniam dicat Hilarius Frumentius . . .* (Rome, 1617). Courtesy of the Biblioteca Casanatense, Rome.

to suit his own needs, his broadsheet must closely resemble the one published by Frumenti seventeen years earlier.[18]

Frumenti's broadsheet was accompanied by a set of six Latin poems published in a separate libretto and handed out to the audience at the same time as the broadsheet.[19] The author of the poems was Padre Cesare Laurenti (1583–1621), a professor of Latin letters at the Roman College and a prolific poet who was often called on to compose verses for doctoral defenses and other public functions of the kind.[20] Laurenti's name appears neither on the title page nor anywhere else in the volume; instead, it is Frumenti who dedicates the volume to Cardinal de' Medici, as though he were the author. This kind of an arrangement was not unusual. Maintaining a fiction of authorial anonymity was standard practice at the Jesuit colleges, where professors spent much of their time writing poems, epigrams, sermons, treatises, and other literary and scientific productions, which their students then presented to the public. The fact that one often finds the name of the real author written in by hand on the title pages of publications of this kind suggests that his identity was never seriously hidden from those who were interested in knowing it.[21]

The same Matthaeus Greuter who designed and engraved the thesis print also designed and engraved the title page of the volume of poems (fig. 6). Within an architectural frame of solomonic columns supporting a broken pediment the title is inscribed on a cloth held by putti. Continuing the theme of the thesis print, the cardinal's coat of arms above is echoed below by a model of the cosmos with the motto *Nihil extra* (Nothing beyond).

The libretto opens with a two-page dedicatory preface, offering a brief synopsis of Medici glory (see the appendix to the introduction). It lists, in chronological order, each of the most illustrious members of the family, from Cosimo and Lorenzo the Magnificent to the dukes and grand dukes of Tuscany, not omitting the Medici popes Leo X and Clement VII or the Medici queens of France, Caterina and Maria. The dedication is followed by the six poems, one for each of the *palle* and entitled "Sol," "Saturnus," "Iuppiter," "Mercurius,"

"Luna," and "Mars," respectively. (Venus, once again, is combined with Apollo in "Sol," a solution that brings with it a twofold advantage, for not only does it lower the number of cosmic spheres from seven to six, it also sidelines Venus, who, as the goddess of love, might otherwise fit uneasily in a panegyric addressed to a cardinal.) Like the thesis print and the dedicatory preface, the poems are blatantly encomiastic in content and combine mythological, allegorical, astrological, and heraldic imagery in homage to Cardinal de' Medici.

Laurenti's sophisticated neo-Latin verses and the problems posed by their adaptation to the musical score are discussed in more detail in the essay by Clare Woods that follows. Here, it need only be emphasized that the engraved broadsheet, the poetry, and the music commissioned for Frumenti's defense constitute a meticulously coordinated artistic program. Each part contributes to the *concetto* in its own particular language—visual, verbal, or musical—but it is only when we experience the parts together that the meaning of the whole emerges. The heavens are transformed into a reflection of Medici glory, and the dedicatee's heraldic *palle*, metamorphosed into planets, become the instruments of celestial harmony that make the music of the spheres.

Courtly imagery of this kind was, of course, a commonplace, and astronomical metaphors in various guises appear repeatedly in the panegyric literature and art surrounding the Medici family.[22] Even scientists played the game. In his *Sidereus nuncius* of 1610, dedicated to Grand Duke Cosimo II, Galileo published, along with his findings on the phases of Venus, his discovery of the moons of Jupiter, which he named the Medicean Stars in honor of his patron.[23] No doubt the astronomer would have preferred that his telescope had revealed six moons instead of the four he actually observed; but even if nature in this instance did not fully cooperate with an heraldic agendum, Galileo seized the opportunity to frame an elegant and enduring compliment to his Medici sponsor.[24] Laurenti seems to allude to Galileo's discovery in the concluding lines to the first of the poems, "Sol," where he substitutes Cardinal Carlo for his brother the grand duke:

> Thus now the name of Carlo gallops
> through the six spheres and is written
> on the deep-blue pages of the gods,
> where it is written forever in the Medicean Stars.
>
> Phoebus sings this to the sky, Phoebus,
> emperor of the stars, who has devised new stars
> that he names after the Medici,
> with Carlo as their prince.[25]

The Galilean reference may not end with the phases of Venus and the moons of Jupiter. The fact that Frumenti's defense took place in 1617 suggests the intriguing possibility that the entire program was conceived in response to the controversy over heliocentrism then raging in Rome, in which Galileo played a central role. Galileo had arrived in the city in December 1615, summoned there to defend his Copernican views against the opposition of conservative voices within the Church, among them the zealous Jesuit Cardinal Roberto Bellarmino. While in Rome Galileo lived in the Villa Medici under the protection of his Florentine patrons. He was warmly received throughout the city, and wherever he went he argued the case for heliocentrism, attacking and ridiculing the official Ptolemaic view of an earth fixed and stationary at the center of the universe. Tact was not his strong point. The Florentine ambassador Piero Guicciardini reported to the grand duke, "he is all afire on his opinions, and puts great passion in them, and not enough strength and prudence in controlling it; so that the Roman climate is getting very dangerous for him."[26] Galileo had his supporters in Rome, among them Cardinal Del Monte, who warned him to lie low and keep his views on heliocentrism to himself; but there was no persuading him.[27] The visit ended, inevitably, in disaster. On 26 February 1616, Galileo was summoned before Cardinal Bellarmino, officially admonished, and instructed to cease and desist from teaching or defending the Copernican theory. One month later, Copernicus was put on the index of prohibited books.[28]

All of this put Cardinal Carlo de' Medici in an extremely awkward position. Arriving in Rome in April 1616, barely a month after the admonition, the newly created cardinal was faced with a perilous conflict of interest. On the one hand, the ties of patronage obligated him to support Galileo, who was, after all, not only a client of the Medici and under their direct protection, but the leading Florentine intellectual of his time and a key player in the cultural politics of the grand duchy. On the other hand, as a prince of the Church, he was duty bound to maintain its doctrines and policies, including its stand against Copernicanism. The Florentine ambassador had already warned the cardinal of the danger to his reputation in associating too freely with Galileo.

> This issue, this affair has now become embarrassing and unwelcome at court; and if, when he arrives here, the Lord Cardinal, as a good ecclesiastic, does not support the deliberations of the Church, according to the will of the pope and of the Congregation of the Holy Office, which is the foundation and basis of religion and the most important congregation in Rome, he will lose a great deal and give considerable displeasure.[29]

The cardinal took the ambassador's warning seriously, and we sense his discomfiture in a letter addressed to Galileo by one of the Medici secretaries shortly after the cardinal's arrival in Rome:

> I understand that you are thinking about staying in Rome as long as Cardinal de' Medici will be there. In this regard I recall what Their Highnesses told me at some point, that is, that I should advise you that when you find yourself at the table of the Lord Cardinal, where other learned people are likely to be as well, Your Lordship should not get into disputations about those matters that have triggered the friars' persecution against you.[30]

Galileo was sure that the cardinal would protect him from his enemies. He wrote to Florence:

> I am confident that the arrival here of the Illustrious and Reverend Cardinal will in itself obviate my need to speak

out in my own defense; his name will answer for me throughout the court.[31]

But Galileo's outspoken advocacy of heliocentrism, which continued despite Bellarmino's admonition, clearly embarrassed Cardinal Carlo, and it is easy to imagine him welcoming any opportunity to distance himself publicly from the scientist's radical views.

Frumenti's defense provided just such an opportunity. Whether astronomy was one of the subjects Frumenti addressed in his disputation we cannot know, since his conclusions have not come down to us. It was central to the artistic program of his defense, however, and the planetary system described in both Greuter's engraving and Laurenti's verses, although expressed in poetic rather than scientific terms, was unmistakably Ptolemaic in its structure. One year after Bellarmino's admonition and the indexing of Copernicus, Frumenti's defense offered a public exhibition of astronomical conformism, in which Cardinal Carlo played his part simply by attending and accepting the dedication to himself. In the great hall of the Roman College, the mother school of the Jesuit order and the intellectual home of Galileo's enemies, Cardinal Carlo allowed his family name to be celebrated in Ptolemaic terms and the Medici *stemma* to be recast as a model of a geocentric cosmos.

As a curious aside, when Fra Giovanni Dalla Torre reused Frumenti's thesis print for his own defense in 1634, the Galilean controversy may once again have been a motivating factor behind the choice of imagery (fig. 5). Dalla Torre was a Dominican friar and his defense took place in the Dominican college at S. Maria sopra Minerva, probably in the very hall where one year earlier, on 22 June 1633, Galileo had appeared before the inquisitors and been forced to recant his claim that the sun is at the center of the universe and the earth in motion around it. Dalla Torre dedicated his conclusions to one of the ten cardinals who had presided over the condemnation of Galileo, Francesco Barberini, and one may wonder whether there was not an intentional irony in his decision to reuse Greuter's engraving. The sycophantic alterations he made to the design illustrate the conceit of a cosmos neither geocentric nor heliocentric in its motions, in which the sun and planets are drawn instead towards a radiant new star that is the embodiment of Barberini glory.[32]

Allegri's Modi *and Roman Defense Music*

The music performed at Frumenti's defense was written and directed by Domenico Allegri (ca. 1585–1629).[33] What is known about the composer is quickly summarized. Like his brothers Gregorio and Bartolomeo, Domenico received his training as a choirboy at S. Luigi dei Francesi in the 1590s, under the direction of Giovanni Bernardino Nanino. After a stint in the provinces, he returned to Rome in 1609 and served briefly as maestro di cappella at S. Maria in Trastevere, before being named to the prestigious post of maestro di cappella of S. Maria Maggiore, which he held from 1610 until his death in 1629. He was twice married (the second time in 1615 to Virginia Vanni, the sister of a singer in the Cappella Sistina) and had five sons and a daughter.[34] Although today overshadowed by his older brother Gregorio (who on account of a certain "Miserere" enjoys a posthumous reputation out of proportion to his accomplishment), Domenico was arguably the more successful of the two and seemed destined for greater fame, had he not died at the relatively early age of forty-four (Gregorio, who was older to begin with, outlived him by another twenty-three years). It is proof of the high regard in which Domenico was held that he was appointed maestro di cappella of S. Maria Maggiore when he was only twenty-five years old.

The fact that Frumenti was able to employ an artist of Allegri's standing to provide the music for his defense is indicative of the importance attached to commissions of this sort. Clearly, music performed at defenses was expected to be of the highest quality, and not only Allegri but most of the leading composers active in Rome in the seventeenth century were involved in its production. Indeed, defense music must have been one of the commonest forms of freelance work available to them. Those securely documented as composers of defense music include Virgilio Mazzocchi,[35] Orazio Benevoli,[36] Carlo Cecchelli,[37] Nicolò Stamegna,[38] and Giuseppe Ottavio Pitoni,[39] but this is only a partial list. Such was the demand for good new music on these occasions that there was probably not a competent choirmaster in the city who was not offered at least some commissions of the kind.

Defense music was not normally printed; Allegri's score for Frumenti's defense may be unique in this respect. We do not know who it was who decided to print the score, but it is unlikely that Allegri himself had much to do with it. He seems to have had little or no interest in disseminating his work through publication, and this is the only one of his compositions known to have been printed in his lifetime. More likely it was Frumenti who came up with the idea, or perhaps one of his Jesuit professors, intending the score as a sophisticated party favor to be handed out to the members of the audience along with the engraved thesis broadsheet and the libretto of poems.

The score's plain title page offers no explanation (fig. 7). Indeed, nowhere in the volume is there any mention of the occasion for which the music was composed or of the student who commissioned it. There is no preface or dedication of any kind, a fact that surprises given the encomiastic program of the defense as a whole. Only the text, drawn from Laurenti's celebratory poems in honor of Carlo de' Medici, connects the music indisputably with Frumenti's defense (figs. 9 and 10).

On the other hand, circumstantial evidence supports the idea that the printed score was indeed meant to be handed out at the defense, along with the broadsheet and the libretto. To begin with, like the libretto it is dated 1617, the year of Frumenti's defense. Moreover, in at least one instance a copy of the score and a copy of the libretto have come down to us bound side by side in a volume of miscellanea, suggesting that whoever originally

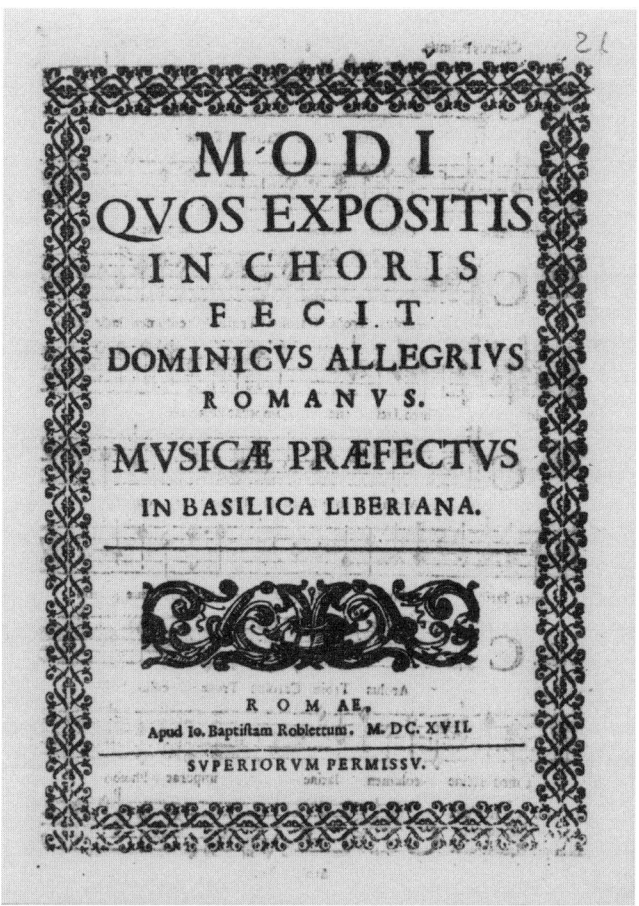

Figure 7. *Modi quos expositis in choris fecit Dominicus Allegrius Romanus Musicae Praefectus in Basilica Liberiana* (Rome, 1617), title page. Courtesy of the Biblioteca Casanatense, Rome.

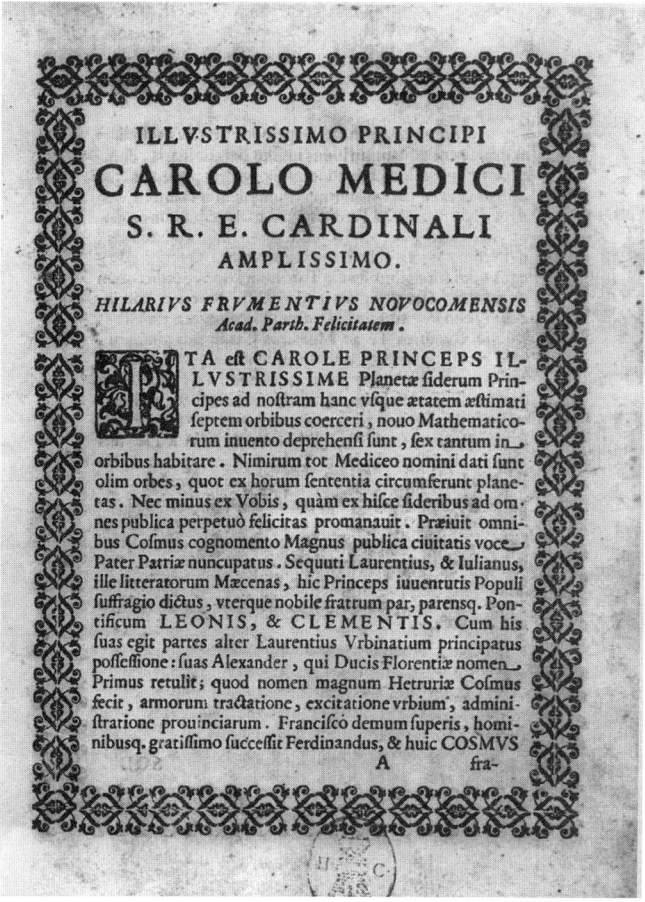

Figure 8. [Cesare Laurenti], *Illustrissimo Principi Carolo Medici . . . Caelestium Orbium Armoniam dicat Hilarius Frumentius . . .* (Rome, 1617), opening page of the dedicatory preface. Courtesy of the Biblioteca Casanatense, Rome.

owned them received both publications at once and kept them always together.[40] We know that the libretto was distributed at the defense; it follows that the score was as well. The score and the libretto were published by different printers, but one would expect this to be the case given the different specializations involved. Giovanni Battista Robletti, one of the leading music printers in Rome, was responsible for the score, while Giacomo Mascardi, a text printer, published the poems. Internal evidence suggests that Robletti and Mascardi (both of whom worked extensively for the Jesuits) collaborated closely in the production of the two booklets.[41] The title page of the score and the dedicatory text of the libretto have identical wood-block borders (figs. 7 and 8). Perhaps one of the printers loaned the other his pieces of woodblock in order to ensure a degree of visual harmony between the two publications or perhaps Mascardi printed the title page of the score; it is not difficult to imagine a scenario whereby the pages requiring the expertise of a music printer were entrusted to Robletti, whereas the pages exclusively of text—including the title page of the score—were turned over to the typographer Mascardi. However it came about, it is clear that a considerable degree of coordination was involved.

Turning now to Allegri's score, we confront the question of its genre. The terminology used in the seventeenth century to describe the choral music composed for academic defenses tends to be vague and inconsistent. Sometimes the pieces are simply called "songs" (*carmina, cantus, odae, meloi*) or "choruses" (*chori*), sometimes "motets," "cantatas," or "madrigals." Beginning in the late 1630s, the term *melodramma* is occasionally used. The title to Allegri's score for Frumenti's defense resorts to the generic word *modi* (meaning measures, i.e., music); whereas Giuseppe Ottavio Pitoni, writing later in the century, refers to Allegri's composition as a cantata. We might call such works secular motets, or more precisely, since their function is essentially celebratory and encomiastic, dedicatory motets.

Allegri's score consists of three movements, with texts excerpted from three of Laurenti's six poems. As we have already seen, at a typical defense there were choral interludes at three or four key moments. Thus Allegri's arrangement corresponds perfectly to what we know of performance practice. We can imagine Frumenti's defense unfolding as follows. At the outset, as the broadsheet, libretto, and score were being distributed and as the audience was admiring the engraving for the first time, the choirs sang the opening chorus, "Sol." The second chorus, "Saturnus," followed Frumenti's dedicatory speech in praise of his patron. The disputation then took

Figure 9. *Modi quos expositis in choris fecit Dominicus Allegrius Romanus Musicae Praefectus in Basilica Liberiana* (Rome, 1617), opening measures of "Sol." Courtesy of the Biblioteca Casanatense, Rome.

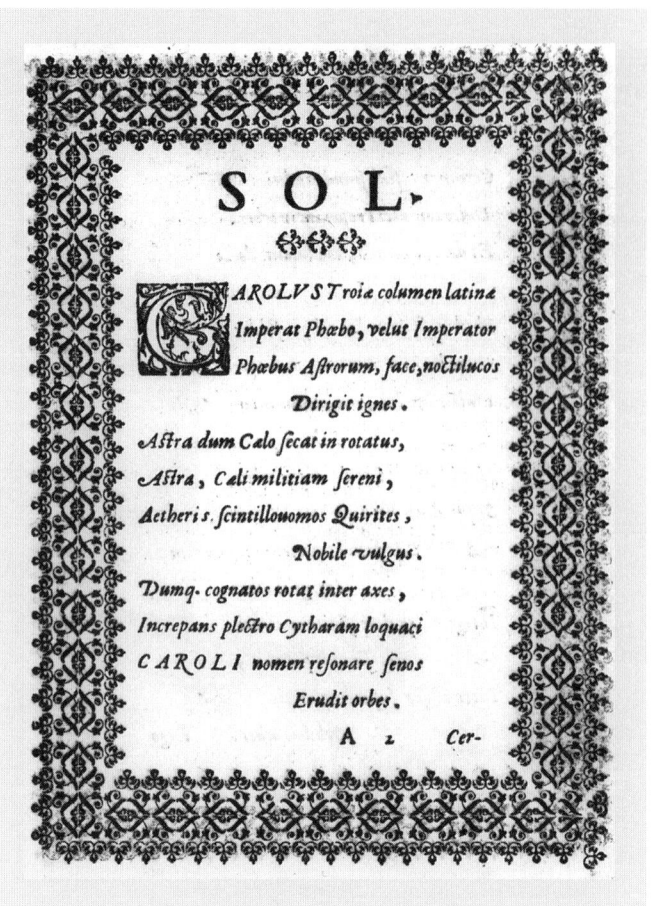

Figure 10. [Cesare Laurenti], *Illustrissimo Principi Carolo Medici ... Caelestium Orbium Armoniam dicat Hilarius Frumentius ...* (Rome, 1617), opening lines of "Sol." Courtesy of the Biblioteca Casanatense, Rome.

place. The third and final movement, "Mercurius," was performed at the triumphal conclusion of the defense and functioned as an applause-trigger, as its emphatically capitalized last line makes plain: "IAM PLAUSU CAELUM STETIT IMPAR" (now the sky could not contain the applause). This is the shortest of the three movements, and its brevity may, once again, reflect common practice. By the time the last section of a defense motet was performed, the audience had been sitting still for quite a while and was likely restless. A final chorus that went on too long ran the risk of being cut short, as happened at a defense at the Sapienza that took place on a steamy July day in 1666, when the rector of the university, conscious of the constraints of time and fearing also that the singers' breath was raising the temperature in the room beyond what was tolerable, decided on the spur of the moment to abridge the concluding choral movement.[42] Allegri, careful not to overtax his audience's attention span, kept his last movement brief and to the point.

Defense librettos survive in large numbers, but unfortunately the texts they contain, although clearly meant to be sung, offer few hints as to their musical treatment. The fact that, in Frumenti's case, we have both the libretto and the score allows us to study the relationship between text and music and to deduce from it aspects of performance practice that we can then apply to the many other librettos for which scores do not survive. For example, defense librettos from the first third of the seventeenth century rarely differentiate between solo and choral sections and one might therefore assume that there was no solo singing at these events, were it not for the evidence of Frumenti's defense. His libretto, too, gives no indication of solo singing, yet the score is filled with it. The soloists do not have separate arias, but short sections—solos, duets, quartets, etc.—woven into the larger choral framework. This seems to have been standard practice, and beginning around the middle of the 1630s the librettos begin to reflect it, distinguishing between choruses and character roles sung by soloists, just as one would expect to find in the librettos for oratorios or operas.

Some defense librettos contain a single poem, others three or four, still others half a dozen or more. Frumenti's example teaches us that the number of poems in a libretto is an unreliable indicator of the number of musical movements performed during a defense. His libretto includes six poems, but only three were set to music, or, to be more specific, excerpts of three; in other words, considerably less than half of Laurenti's text was actually sung. It would appear that composers were not obliged to set every line of verse entrusted to them and could divide or subdivide the poems as they saw fit. Indeed, they could make other changes as well, and the text to Allegri's score is full of minor departures from the wording of Laurenti's libretto, some of which no doubt resulted from faulty transcription, but others of which were apparently intentional emendations introduced for the purpose of adapting the text to the melodic line.

Heraldry features prominently in most defense librettos, and it is likely that the symbols of nobility that permeate the poetic texts found expression in the music as well. There are precedents for the musical portrayal of a patron's coat of arms in secular celebratory music from at least the fifteenth century. Among pieces dedicated to the Medici one could cite Heinrich Isaac's canzona "Palle, palle" (ca. 1484–94), Andrea de Silva's motet "Gaude felix Florentia" (ca. 1513), and a puzzle-canon written by Giovanni Maria Nanino in 1605 on the occasion of the election of Pope Leo XI de' Medici. Each of these works has been shown to contain musical depictions of the Medici coat of arms, rendered as a series of notes that rise and fall symmetrically.[43] Allegri's score contains no such obvious armorial figures, but the heraldic motif of the ball (*palla*) is treated with particular emphasis. In the first movement, for example, where the tenor sings, "Ergo iam senos equitat per orbes Caroli nomen" (thus the name of Carlo now gallops through the six spheres), the composer stresses the word "orbes" much as he does the name "Caroli," repeating it and stretching it out in ornamental runs of notes. To judge from other librettos, heraldic game-playing in various guises was a common feature of music for the academic defense.

In other respects, defense music seems to have followed contemporary developments in choral music generally. It is clear from the surviving texts that it displayed many of the favorite devices of polychoral composers, who loved to play off one chorus against the other, sometimes introducing mock battles or competitions between them, sometimes setting up echo effects, with one choir echoing the other.[44] As the century progressed, music for the defense grew larger in scale and more dramatic in content. Soloists were assigned character roles, and the music—again, to judge from the surviving librettos—took on narrative qualities suggesting close parallels with oratorio and opera. The term *melodramma*, used as early as the 1630s to describe music written for a defense, underscores the theatrical nature of these pieces and the interconnectedness of art, poetry, and music in the spectacle surrounding the disputation.

Of the numerous motets written for and performed in Roman defenses between the end of the sixteenth century and the middle of the eighteenth century, Allegri's score for the defense of Ilario Frumenti may be the sole survivor. The loss of virtually every other work in this category has meant that the importance of the defense in the musical life of the city has until now been largely overlooked. Allegri's *Modi* opens a window onto this unfamiliar chapter in music history. Festive and rousing, it brings vividly to life the triumphant pageantry of the academic defense in baroque Rome.

Poetry into Song: Lyrics for a Thesis Defense, *by Clare Woods*

The Jesuit poet Cesare Laurenti composed six poems, "Sol," "Saturnus," "Iuppiter," "Mercurius," "Luna," and "Mars," for the occasion of Ilario Frumenti's thesis defense. Each is named for a Greco-Roman god, but given the prominence accorded to Sol/Phoebus, it seems likely that the divine hierarchy is astrological rather than purely Olympian.[1] Laurenti has modified the astrological scheme slightly, however: the six *palle* of the Medici device necessitated six poems, where astrologically we might have expected seven.[2] Venus does not receive a poem, and yet Laurenti has not excluded her altogether: we learn from the closing section of Mars' poem, and can also see in the design of the thesis print, that, greedy for the Sun's light, she has joined him in his chariot.[3] Where the setting is earthly, Laurenti presents a classicizing landscape: the city of Rome, decked out for a triumph as in "Saturnus"; or hints of a bucolic scene in "Mercurius," replete with nymphs and sirens. Within this pagan world of mythical creatures, divine opulence, and awe-inspiring majesty, Laurenti sets his Medici patrons.

Of Laurenti's six poems, Allegri selected excerpts from three—"Sol," "Saturnus," and "Mercurius"—for musical treatment. Each of these is composed in a different classical meter.[4] More detailed analysis of Laurenti's text reveals further debts to classical and late ancient Latin poets. In the texts selected for the song lyrics, for example, we find Laurenti weaving into his own work phrases borrowed from Horace, Catullus, Ausonius, and Prudentius.[5] His poems thus have a rich, layered quality: they exhibit not only their author's erudition, but also allow the educated reader to derive further pleasure from recognizing allusions to earlier literature. One other feature of Laurenti's Latin style worth noting here is his liking for unusual and obscure vocabulary. The exotic instruments mentioned in "Mercurius" provide a striking example, and these may well have been culled from grammatical treatises or lexica.[6] Laurenti, however, also uses words that appear to be his own coinages: for example, *scintillivomos* (literally, spark-spewing), *caeris* (possibly a combination of *ceris* [wax tablets] and *caeruleis* [sky-blue]), both in "Sol"; and *nubifidas* (cloud-trusting) in "Mercurius."[7]

In selecting material for the songs, much of Laurenti's original poetry was cut, and the lyrics betray this with somewhat abrupt transitions from one theme to the next. As will become apparent, the message of the songs becomes clearer only if one also has access to Laurenti's original poems, which were circulated at Frumenti's thesis defense (see Louise Rice's essay above). The following section discusses the relationship between the songs and the original poems, sketching in the content of the originals and noting any alterations made to the text in shaping it for musical performance.

"Sol" (The Sun): Only the first two and the last two stanzas of the original nine have been set to music, and, while the basic structure of the whole has been retained, the third stanza of the musical setting arrives rather abruptly.[8] The opening "Ergo" (Thus) of this stanza makes better sense in its original context, following five stanzas that have introduced and developed the theme of six celestial spheres and their correspondence to the Medici device. Nevertheless, the motet text contains the kernel of the original poem's message: Carlo is the greatest luminary in town, rather like Phoebus lording it over the other stars.[9] And because the newly discovered satellites of Jupiter have been dedicated to the Medici, Carlo's name, so our poet argues, is effectively written eternally in the stars.

"Saturnus" (Saturn): Only thirteen lines from the original thirty-three have been set to music, and with certain key lines lost, it is difficult to understand how the lyrics relate to Saturn. Toward the end of the original poem, however, the context makes it clear that all of the preceding lines have been Saturn's song, his contribution to the proceedings. These final lines also include a reference to the so-called Golden Age: a mythical age of prosperity and ease governed by Saturn. In the poem Saturn promises Carlo an age like his own, fashioned in pure gold.[10] The original poem also contains a fuller eulogy of Rome, which with its Catullan meter and vocabulary has the flavor of a love song in praise of the city—appropriate perhaps, since later lines present Rome as Carlo's bride.[11] Lines 11 and 12 of the motet text refer to another city, the Medici's own Florence. In Laurenti's poem the relationship between Rome and Florence is developed to suggest that with Carlo wedded to Rome and with Florence wedded to the Medici, Rome and Florence are effectively consorts, exchanging hills for spheres. The musical setting retains none of this imagery. Instead, perhaps to make the reference to Florence stand out better in the two lines allotted to the city, the original text has been adjusted from "cor virentis orbis" (heart of the verdant world) to "flos virentis orbis" (flower of the verdant world), a patterning of sounds surely designed to evoke Florence at the close of the song.[12]

"Mercurius" (Mercury): Allegri uses a mere twelve lines from the original forty-seven and adjusts the text to present a message completely opposite to that conveyed in the original poem. The crux of the difference lies in the removal of the verb *sistite*, a command to cease action, with the result that a succession of phrases in the song involving instruments and the sounds they make is now governed by *tundite*, a verb that creates noise rather than quells it. The original poem had addressed and then silenced in turn a large and exotic assembly of musicians and instruments. In the interest of removing all extraneous noise, Laurenti had even specifically banished the nymph Echo.[13] This poem was to be a solo piece for Mercury alone, accompanying himself on his lyre. Allegri's setting of the poem invites noise, however, and the song enjoys a brief musical tour through a range of string and percussion instruments before stopping to admire the echo and comment, optimistically, on the level of subsequent applause.

In producing this edition, we needed to address the fact that there are textual differences between the original poems and the lyrics as they appear in the printed music. These differences appear to have arisen for a variety of reasons, and it did not seem appropriate either to restore the original text wholesale or to adopt unquestioningly the readings in the musical version. For brevity's sake, rather than analyze each point of difference, I will present one or two examples of the types of problems encountered and state the principles used in establishing the musical text.

That the original text was deliberately altered in shaping the musical setting is clear from the discussion above. We have already noted the substitution of *flos* for *cor* in "Saturnus"; other examples where variants constitute viable readings in the context of the song include *iusta* (fitting) for *fausta* (auspicious), and *superba* (proud) for *subacta* (conquered). The latter, in reference to Rome, may have had more appeal for a Roman audience! Other textual changes were more pragmatic in that, in terms of syllables, the new reading better fits the musical line. Two instances from "Mercurius" illustrate this point: *neque* instead of the original *non* (line 1); and, clearly part of a larger change already discussed above, *et concordes* instead of *sistite molles* (line 7).

The song lyrics, however, contain a number of readings that are clearly errors, whether just simple slips, perhaps in the typesetting—*roboantes* for *reboantes*, for example, or *dominus* for *dominos*—or more serious mistakes, where the original poetry has been rendered as a string of nonsense words.[14] The most dramatic example of the latter occurs in "Mercurius," lines 4–6, where we find in the music: "Huic ergo compescita vestros / Compita lutus palpita plausus, / Rumpite mores nobila palma." Although these lines may sound like Latin, *compescita* and *nobila* are grammatically impossible, and *lutus, palpita, mores,* and *palma* exist as Latin words, but make little or no sense in this context. One explanation for the large number of mistakes might be that the music was somewhat hurriedly prepared, especially in the case of "Mercurius," the final piece, and that lyrics were copied into the parts by someone with a limited knowledge of Latin or at least of Laurenti's more unusual vocabulary. One might of course argue, in the absence of any other evidence, that the music was performed as is, nonsense and all. Nevertheless, although our primary aim is to reconstruct the music as it might have been performed, it is clearly desirable to present a coherent text, and therefore, where the lyrics make no sense at all, they have been emended with the help of Laurenti's original poems.

Performance Practice, *by Antony John*

Like the German College and other colleges throughout Rome, the Roman College had a choir composed of students who, aged from roughly eleven to twenty-three years, would have covered all four vocal parts. How many singers comprised this choir we do not know, although at Frumenti's defense there would likely have been only one or two singers per part. Professional singers might have been brought in from some of the major churches (quite possibly including S. Maria Maggiore, where Allegri was employed as maestro di cappella) to strengthen the ensemble and to perform the solo sections, as was common practice with festive occasions in Roman churches.[1] Greater skill and versatility on the part of the soloist is suggested by the slight extension of the otherwise restricted ambitus and other technical demands in the sections for soloists (e.g., "Sol," mm. 56–77). The designations "solus," "solum," and "voc. 8" may have served to give performers advance notice of the texture of a section, rather than indicating a specific number of singers. Since the source is not consistent in providing solo indications, some passages have been editorially assigned to soloists according to the vocal texture (e.g., "Saturnus," mm. 38–54).

The two choirs should be clearly separated as was the custom in baroque Rome, where the construction of additional choir platforms often allowed for a wider distribution of choral groups throughout a building in polychoral works (as described in the essay by Louise Rice above).[2] It is quite likely that two such platforms were constructed (or owned outright) by the Roman College for occasions such as these. Given the size of the main hall in the Roman College, the platforms, placed against the walls on either side, would have been at least thirty feet apart.

As noted in the critical report, an interesting feature of the source is the presence of Latin rubrics indicating additional accompanying instruments—for example, "cum plena vocum instrumentorumque concencione" (with the full harmony of voices and instruments) and "cum plena instrum. Symph." (with the full ensemble of instruments) —although no parts for them are provided anywhere; the instrumental parts in this edition are editorial reconstructions. All but one of the rubrics specifically mention strings or violins ("fidib[us]"). Nevertheless, a single rubric at the beginning of "Saturnus" ("s[ine] A[ulos],"without winds) suggests the possibility that references to the "full ensemble" may imply additional instruments, such as recorders, cornetts, and/or trombones. A modern performance could certainly include the addition of appropriate instruments.

Allegri's continuo part (marked "Org.") is a *basso seguente* throughout the tutti choral sections.[3] Although only an organ is explicitly indicated, it is possible that a theorbo, lute, or harpsichord may have shared the continuo part, depending on the extent of the choral forces employed.[4] In the source the continuo part is not figured (as was often the case in this period); to facilitate performance, full editorial figures have been added in the present edition.[5] The realization of the continuo must take into account the size of the chorus, as doubtless was the case in early performances of the work.[6] Furthermore, the realization likely would have been kept simple in the full-voice segments but made more elaborate in segments with a thinner vocal texture.[7]

The alternation of triple and duple meters characteristic of this period is in evidence throughout the work, consistently indicated as O3 and C, respectively, which could indicate a relationship of three semibreves in triple meter to either one semibreve or two semibreves in duple;[8] the equivalency formulas given in this edition suggest the former relationship. For the segments in duple meter, we have found that a traditional, moderate tactus of MM 60–70 per minim proves workable in each of the movements.[9] Although the evidence suggests that pitch in early-seventeenth-century Rome was comparatively lower than today (possibly as low as $a' = 384$), performance of the work at $a' = 440$ is desirable, as transposing down will result in an especially low bass line.[10]

Appendix

Dedicatory Preface in [Cesare Laurenti], *Illustrissimo Principi Carolo Medici . . . Caelestium Orbium Armoniam dicat Hilarius Frumentius . . .* **(Rome, 1617)**

TO THE MOST ILLUSTRIOUS PRINCE | CARLO DE' MEDICI | MOST DISTINGUISHED CARDINAL OF THE HOLY ROMAN CHURCH. | ILARIO FRUMENTI OF COMO | of the Parthenian Academy [wishes] good fortune.

Thus it is, most illustrious Prince Carlo, that the planets, the princes of the stars, considered until our own time to be enclosed in seven spheres, have been found in a new discovery of the astronomers to dwell only in six spheres. Without doubt, in their opinion, as many spheres clothe the planets as were once given to the Medici name. And no less from you than from these very stars has universal happiness emanated continuously for all. Cosimo, named the Great, preceded all and was called Father of the Fatherland by universal acclaim of the state. Lorenzo and Giuliano followed, the former a Maecenas for the learned, the latter styled a Prince of the People, winning the vote of the young; both brothers were equally noble, both the parent of popes [namely] Leo and Clement. Alongside these another Lorenzo played his part with the acquisition of the principality of Urbino; and Alessandro his [part], who was the first to adopt the title of Duke of Florence, a title that Cosimo made Grand [Duke] of Tuscany by use of arms, by rousing up the towns, and by management of the provinces. At length and most pleasingly to gods and men, Ferdinando succeeded Francesco, and your brother Cosimo succeeded him; with regard to Cosimo, we his contemporaries marvel at how much the people's love and zeal for their prince and how much his own benevolence and care for them vie with each other: posterity will rank him alongside the best of princes. Indeed I would have compared you here to your father Ferdinando, whose prudence in ruling this age has admired, and whose power no enemy could disregard. How many times at sea on their decorated triremes did the deadly crescent of the Turks seem to suffer eclipse when confronted with the Medici spheres! I would have done this—I say this not ungratefully—if you had not already, from that great height of purpled majesty, joined yourself to the many Medici cardinals, and to no fewer than four Medici popes. This too should not be credited to a remote branch of your family: that France also added herself to the Medici spheres and planted her lilies on them with a wealth of better fortune, which afterwards Caterina and Maria, each a queen of France, nourished abundantly with their virtues. All these things ought indeed to have had Paolo Giovio as their herald, once held worthy to receive the thrice-twinned Medici orbs. But in desiring this I ought to succeed him not so much as herald but as admirer—if I am connected to him by birth, I should not be severed from him in discharging this duty of praise. And indeed, may this [defense] of my three years' Philosophy, approaching you with this sheaf of propositions, be a contribution to Medici glory. Farewell.

Translation by Clare Woods

Notes

The Philosophy Defense of Ilario Frumenti, *by Louise Rice*

The following sigla are used in these notes:

ACG   Archivio del Collegio Germanico et Ungarico, Rome
AEC   Archives of the English College, Rome
APUG   Archivio della Pontificia Università Gregoriana, Rome
ARSI   Archivum Romanum Societatis Iesu, Rome
ASR   Archivio di Stato, Rome
BAV   Biblioteca Apostolica Vaticana, Rome

1. APUG, no. 2801, p. 505.
2. BAV, Urb. Lat. 1082, fol. 460.
3. APUG, no. 142, fol. 95; cited in Riccardo Garcia Villoslada, *Storia del Collegio Romano dal suo inizio (1551) alla soppressione della Compagnia di Gesù (1773)* (Rome: apud aedes Universitatis Gregorianae, 1954), 270.
4. For more on this subject, see Louise Rice, "Jesuit Thesis Prints and the Festive Academic Defence at the Collegio Romano," in *The Jesuits: Cultures, Sciences, and the Arts, 1540–1773*, ed. John O'Malley, et al. (Toronto: University of Toronto Press, 1999), 148–69; and idem, "Pietro da Cortona and the Roman Baroque Thesis Print," in *Pietro da Cortona, 1597–1669: Atti del convegno internazionale . . . 1997*, ed. Christoph Luitpold Frommel and Sebastian Schütze (Milan: Electa, 1998), 189–200.
5. "Si cantorno cose nuove in lode del Cardinale [Paravicino], quale restò contentissimo. . . . Si cantò 4 volte: in principio, dopo la Prefatione, dopo le Dispute, e doppo l'Attione di gratie." ACG, Hist. 104, p. 43.
6. "[Li Signori Cardinali et il detto Signor Principe] a coppia, secondo l'antianità, passarono [alla sala] delle dispute. Li musici diedero subito principio alla sinfonia degl'istrumenti, et alla melodia delle voci, cantando la prima ode de' versi latini . . . ; e tanto durarono, fin che commodamente da dui gentilhuomini della Casa Altemps manierosi e discreti fuorno dalli dui lati distribuiti li fiori alli Signori Cardinali, Prelati, et altri, alli primi di seta, agli altri odoriferi. Terminato il canto, Monsignore . . . principiò la sua Attione con una Prefatione assai erudita, e molto bene aggiustata, che poi proseguì con lo spiegamento di un testo canonico. . . . Qui fu dai musici cantata l'ode seconda, mentre nell'istesso tempo si distribuirono le conclusioni. . . . Terminata la distributione, si sentirono tre Arguenti, e . . . a gli argomenti di essi, et alle reiterate repliche rispose con molta franchezza il Difendente, con portare nel fine di ciascuno argomento li fondamenti della conclusione. Terminata la disputa, il coro de' musici cantò la terza et ultima ode, mentre nel medesimo tempo si fece la distributione delle compositioni cantate, stampate in libro." ASR, Cartari-Febei, vol. 80, fols. 193r–193v; partially transcribed in Arnaldo Morelli, "La musica a Roma nella seconda metà del Seicento attraverso l'archivio Cartari-Febei," in *La musica a Roma attraverso le fonti d'archivio: Atti del convegno internazionale . . . 1992*, ed. Bianca Maria Antolini, Arnaldo Morelli, and Vera Vita Spagnuolo (Lucca: Libreria musicale italiana, 1994), 121.
7. On seventeenth-century Roman polychoral music, see *La scuola policorale romana del Sei-Settecento: Atti del convegno internazionale di studi in memoria di Laurence Feininger*, ed. Francesco Luisi, et al. (Trent: Servizio beni librari e archivistici, 1997).
8. "Ci furno sei cardinal con molti altri prelati e con buona musica, ma senza organo ne altri istrumenti, et un solo palco." ACG, Hist. 104, p. 43.
9. [3 September 1614], "Il giorno dopo pranzo nel Colleggio Romano D. Francesco de Guevara figliolo del Duca di Bovino sostenne le sue publiche conclusioni di Filosofia nella prima sala a capo della scala parata richissimamente, con 4 cori di musica numerosa d'instromenti et voci elette." BAV, Urb. Lat. 1082, fol. 460.
10. [1639], "In Collegio Romano furono diffese solenni conclusioni da Bernardo Barbi da Trento dedicate all'Arciduca Ferdinando Carlo d'Austria . . . con sei chori di musica." APUG, no. 2801, p. 948.
11. "Vi fu una musica ad 8 chori dove cantarono le voci più scelte di Roma, ed oltre questi due chori d'istromenti distinti tra quali vi furono 4 trombe che suonavano d'accordo con l'organo, cosa rare volte udita. Due di queste trombe suona-

vano da quella fenestra che dall'habitazione dei Padri corrisponde in sala." ARSI, Rom. 242, fol. 91.

12. [1693], "A piè del Salone si fece un gran palco, dove erano sopra a 60 istrumenti, che fecero superbissima sinfonia." APUG, no. 142, fol. 99; cited in Garcia Villoslada, *Storia del Collegio Romano*, 271.

13. On Cardinal de' Medici's art patronage, see Elena Fumagalli, "La villa Médicis au XVIIe siècle," in *La Villa Médicis*, vol. 2, *Etudes*, ed. André Chastel and Philippe Morel (Rome: Académie de France à Rome, Ecole française de Rome, 1991), 568–83; and idem, "Guido Reni e il Cardinale Carlo de' Medici," *Paragone* 45 (1994): 240–46.

14. For example, Francesco Maria del Riccio, a Florentine student at the Roman College, dedicated his theses to Cardinal de' Medici in 1619, as did the Pisan Francesco Rosselmini, also at the Roman College, in 1625.

15. On Paolo Giovio, see T. C. Price Zimmermann, *Paolo Giovio: The Historian and the Crisis of Sixteenth-Century Italy* (Princeton: Princeton University Press, 1995). A connection between the Giovio and Frumenti families existed at least as far back as the 1530s, when Paolo Giovio employed Francesco Frumenti as his banker.

16. This is not an unusual situation. Thesis broadsheets rarely survive in one piece. Because of their large size (they were often more than a meter in height), they were difficult to store and tended to be damaged over time and eventually discarded. The prints that decorated them, on the other hand, were highly prized and were often saved when the rest was thrown away.

17. The conceit is spelled out in the opening line of the dedicatory preface to the accompanying poems (see note 19 below): "Thus it is, most illustrious Prince Carlo, that the planets, the princes of the stars, considered until our own time to be contained in seven spheres, have been found in a new discovery of the astronomers to dwell in only six spheres. Without doubt, in their opinion, as many spheres enclose the planets as were once given to the Medici name." In other words, whereas previously it had been believed that the seven celestial bodies were attached to seven concentric spheres with Earth at their center, now, since it has been demonstrated that Venus orbits the Sun and cannot therefore be attached to a sphere of its own, the seven planetary spheres have been reduced to six, the very number of the balls in the Medici coat of arms.

18. When a student reused an existing thesis print, he often had certain details of the composition altered to conform to his own requirements. In this case Dalla Torre replaced the Medici arms with those of his sponsor, Cardinal Francesco Barberini, and Florence with a different city altogether, perhaps his hometown Lucca. Curiously, this later state of the print bears the signature not only of Matthaeus Greuter, the engraver, but also of the Bolognese painter Baltassare Croce, who is identified as the designer. Croce's name does not appear in the original state.

19. [Cesare Laurenti], *Illustrissimo Principi Carolo Medici S. R. E. Cardinali Magni Ducis Etruriae Fratri Caelestium Orbium Armoniam dicat Hilarius Frumentius Novocomensis Academicus Parthenius dum theses ex Universa Philosophia eidem cardinali inscriptas publice defendit in aula Collegi Romani Societatis Iesu* (Rome: Giacomo Mascardi, 1617; hereafter cited as *Caelestium Orbium Armonia*).

20. In addition to the verses he wrote for Frumenti's defense, Laurenti produced poetry for the thesis defenses of John Lea in 1608 (dedicated to Cardinal Roberto Bellarmino), Stefano Berruti in 1613 (dedicated to Cardinal Giovanni Battista Deti), Tommaso Dralli also in 1613 (dedicated to Cardinal Pietro Aldobrandini), Ambrogio de' Magistris in 1616 (dedicated to Cardinal Scipione Borghese), Albert Swieneicki in 1616 (dedicated to Prince Lorenz Gembicki), Michelangelo Tonti in 1617 (dedicated to Cardinal Borghese), Francesco Maria del Riccio in 1619 (dedicated to Cardinal de' Medici), and Azzone Ariosto in 1621 (dedicated to Pope Gregory XV). In each case, the poetry was published anonymously. For a partial list of Laurenti's published poetry, see the bibliography of his works in Carlos Sommervogel, *Bibliothèque de la Compagnie de Jésus*, 11 vols. (Brussels and Paris, 1890–1932), s.v. "Laurenti, Cesare" (vol. 4, cols. 1565–66).

21. For a copy of Frumenti's libretto with Laurenti's name handwritten on the title page, see Rome, Biblioteca Nazionale Centrale, 34.7.E.3, no. 2.

22. One thinks, for example, of the famous planetary rooms in the Pitti Palace, frescoed by Pietro da Cortona between 1641 and 1665 with depictions of Venus, Apollo, Mars, Jupiter, and Saturn. See Malcolm Campbell, *Pietro da Cortona at the Pitti Palace: A Study of the Planetary Rooms and Related Projects* (Princeton: Princeton University Press, 1977), esp. 144–57.

23. Galileo Galilei, *Sidereus nuncius* (Venice, 1610); translated and edited by Stillman Drake in *Discoveries and Opinions of Galileo* (New York: Anchor Books, 1957), 21–58.

24. See the fascinating discussion in Mario Biagioli, *Galileo, Courtier: The Practice of Science in the Culture of Absolutism* (Chicago: University of Chicago Press, 1993), esp. 121–57.

25. "Ergo iam senos equitat per orbes / CAROLI nomen, superumque caeris / Scribitur, qua Mediceis perenne / Scribitur astris. // Phoebus hoc Caelo canit, Imperator / Phoebus astrorum, nova machinatus / CAROLO quae Principe MEDICIS co[-] / gnominat astra." *Caelestium Orbium Armonia*, [5].

26. Galileo Galilei, *Le opere*, ed. Antonio Favaro, 20 vols. in 21 (Florence, 1890–1909), 12:242, no. 1185; cited in translation in Giorgio De Santillana, *The Crime of Galileo* (Chicago: University of Chicago Press, 1955), 116.

27. De Santillana, ibid., 119.

28. Ibid., 110–44.

29. Letter to the grand duke, 14 March 1616, "Questo punto, questa cosa, hoggi nella Corte è vergognosa et aborrita; et se il Signor Cardinale nella sua venuta qua, come buono ecclesiastico, non mostra ancor lui di non si opporre alle deliberazioni della Chiesa, non seconda la voluntà del Papa et d'una Congregazione come quella del Santo Offizio, che è il fondamento et la base della religione et la più importante di Roma, perderà assai e darà gran disgusto." Galileo, *Opere*, 12:242.

30. Galileo, ibid., 18:422, no. 1198bis; cited in translation in Biagioli, *Galileo, Courtier*, 168.

31. Letter to Curzio Picchena in Florence, 6 March 1616, "[S]on sicurissimo che la sola venuta qua dell'Illustrissimo et Reverendissimo Signor Cardinale mi leverà il bisogno di dover pure fare una parola; tal nome sentirà di me per tutta questa corte." Galileo, *Opere*, 12:245, no. 1187.

32. Dalla Torre defended in theology, and his conclusions have nothing to do with astronomy. For more on the politics of the Copernican controversy as seen through the lens of seventeenth-century prints, see William Ashworth, "Divine Reflections and Profane Refractions: Images of a Scientific Impasse in Seventeenth-Century Italy," in *Gianlorenzo Bernini: New Aspects of His Art and Thought*, ed. Irving Lavin (University Park, Penn.: Pennsylvania State University Press, 1985), 180–207.

33. *Modi quos expositis in choris fecit Dominicus Allegrius Romanus Musicae Praefectus in Basilica Liberiana* (Rome: Giovanni Battista Robletti, 1617). On Allegri, see Giuseppe Ottavio Pitoni, *Notitia de' contrapuntisti e compositori di musica*, ed. Cesarino Ruini (Florence: L. S. Olschki, 1988), 219–20; *The New Grove Dictionary of Music and Musicians*, 2d ed., s.v. "Allegri, Domenico," by Colin Timms; and *Die Musik in Geschichte und Gegenwart*, 2d ed., Personenteil, s.v. "Allegri, Domenico," by Gunther Morche.

34. Jean Lionnet, "The Career of Gregorio Allegri," in the notes to the compact disc Gregorio Allegri, *Miserere, Messe, Motets*, A Sei Voci, Astrée Auvidis E 8524.

35. Virgilio Mazzocchi provided the music for at least two defenses at the English College, one in 1634 and the other in 1646. See Graham Dixon, "Music in the Venerable English College in the Early Baroque," in *La musica a Roma*, 477, citing AEC, busta 999, ricevute 1634, and busta 1001, ricevute 1646 (13 October 1646).

36. Orazio Benevoli composed music for the philosophy defense of a student at the English College in 1649; see Dixon, ibid., citing AEC, busta 1002, ricevute 1649 (3 September 1649).

37. "L'anno 1642 alle 14 decembre . . . Giovanni Giacomo Meiero Germano tenne publicamente le conclusioni di tutta la Filosofia nella sala del Seminario Romano. . . . Fu per trattenimento intermezzata la difesa con una dolce musica composta dal Maestro di Cappella del Seminario con l'intervento de' musici forestieri e primi di quest'alma città di Roma." ARSI, Rom. 242, fol. 71. The maestro di cappella of the Roman Seminary in 1642 was Carlo Cecchelli. Casimiri gives 1645–47 as the dates of Cecchelli's tenure as maestro di cappella of the Seminary in his " 'Disciplina musicae' e 'mastri di capella' nel Seminario Romano (sec. XVI–XVII)," *Note d'archivio per la storia musicale* 15 (1938): 99; but see APUG, no. 2801, p. 1022, which records a performance at the Seminary in 1642 of "una musica molto soave e vaga fatta dal Maestro di Capella Carlo Cecchello."

38. Nicolò Stamegna composed the music for the 1666 law defense of Cristoforo Lozano, a student at the Sapienza. See ASR, Cartari-Febei, vol. 80, fols. 256r–256v; partially transcribed in Morelli, "La musica a Roma . . . attraverso l'archivio Cartari-Febei," 121.

39. Giuseppe Ottavio Pitoni (1657–1743) was maestro di cappella at the German College from 1686 until his death. See Pitoni, *Notitia*, esp. 351–56.

40. Rome, Biblioteca Casanatense, vol. misc. 310, int. 23 and 24.

41. It is possible that when Robletti retired from the music printing business in 1650 he sold his fonts to Mascardi's heir Vitale Mascardi, who started printing music in that very year. If so, it may be indicative of a long-standing relationship between the two publishing houses. I am indebted to Stewart Smith for pointing this out to me. He is investigating Robletti's career and his connections with other Roman printers in "Giovanni Battista Robletti: Music Printer in Baroque Rome" (Ph.D. diss., Royal Holloway, London University, in progress).

42. "Terminati gli argomenti, e le risposte etc., si cantò la terza Ode; la quale fu fatta abbrecciata dal Signor Carpani, parendo che crescesse il caldo dalli fiati, e che il tempo fusse breve." ASR, Cartari-Febei, vol. 80, fols. 257r–257v; transcribed in Morelli, "La musica a Roma . . . attraverso l'archivio Cartari-Febei," 121.

43. Allan Atlas, "Heinrich Isaac's *Palle, palle*: A New Interpretation," *Analecta Musicologica* 14 (1974): 17–25; Richard Sherr, "The Medici Coat of Arms in a Motet for Leo X," *Early Music* 15 (1987): 31–35; and Jean Lionnet, "Another Musical Medici Coat of Arms," *Early Music* 15 (1987): 520–21.

44. A modest echo effect is introduced in "Mercurius" in a back-and-forth between the two soprano soloists.

Poetry into Song: Lyrics for a Thesis Defense, *by Clare Woods*

1. The likelihood of an astrological scheme is increased if we consider Frumenti's claim in his dedicatory letter that good fortune for everyone emanates as much from the Medicis as from the planets ("Nec minus ex Vobis, quam ex hisce sideribus ad omnes publica perpetuo felicitas promanauit").

2. The seven astrological luminaries are the Moon, Mercury, Venus, the Sun, Mars, Jupiter, and Saturn; the planets Uranus, Neptune, and Pluto were not discovered until 1781, 1846, and 1930, respectively.

3. "But Venus would have provided further verses, / if, desiring eagerly a greater light, / she had not rushed to Phoebus' orb; / she took herself off to Phoebus' orb / so that from the circling orbs / six might be left, / to be called the Medici orbs" (Plura at Venus pararet, / Nisi maioris lucis auara / Se Phoebeum ferret in orbem / In Phoebeum se tulit orbem / Vt ex rotatis orbibus / Senos linqueret orbes, / Et Mediceos diceret orbes).

4. "Sol" is composed in sapphic stanzas, that is, three lines of lesser sapphic, one line of adonic, thus: ♩♩♩♩♪♩♩♪♩♩♪ × 3 and ♩♩♪♩♪. "Saturnus" is written in phalaecean (hendecasyllabic) meter: ♩♩♩♪♩♪♩♩♪♩♪. "Mercurius" is composed in anapaestic quaternarius (dimeter acatalectic), which is a more flexible meter. The following are examples of possible rhythms: ♪♪♪♩♩♪♪♪♪ or ♪♪♩♪♪♪♩♩♪♪. Of those poems not set to music, "Jupiter" is composed in first asclepiadean; "Luna" in iambic dimeter; and "Mars" has a polymetric scheme.

5. For "Sol," Horace, *Carmina* 4.6, was particularly influential. "Saturnus" employs Catullan meter, and a smattering of Catullan vocabulary, but also draws on Prudentius, *Peristephanon* 10. "Mercurius" borrows text from Ausonius, *Epistulae* 21 to Paulinus of Nola, and reworks lines from Horace, *Carmina* 3.4.

6. The fairly comprehensive list of *-en* instrumentalists—*liticen* (clarion-sounder), *tibicen* (flute-player), and *fidicen* (lutenist)—worked into lines 11–13 of Laurenti's "Mercurius" supports this suggestion.

7. Many more examples could be given, particularly from "Jupiter"; for example, *serpentigero, gemmigeno, aeternifluae*.

8. The poem begins and ends with a reference to Carlo, and both the first and last stanzas are concerned particularly with the relationship between Carlo and Phoebus.

9. The stars are anthropomorphized here as "a celestial army," "Roman citizens" (*Quirites*), and "the noble populace."

10. "The chief luminary of all sings these things, / Saturn, the old man of the glittering heavens, . . ."

11. For example, lines 5 and 8–9: "Darling of the world, quintessential city . . . citadel of love, sole channel of charms" (Orbis delicium, Urbium medulla . . . arx amorum, Leporum unica vena).

12. We might also note the penultimate line of "Saturnus": "Mera Medicei medulla mellis" (Pure essence of Medicean honey). This is one of the most alliterative of the collection, cleverly providing further emphasis of the Medici association with Florence.

13. "And let not Echo, who wounds words, / and harvests them with utterance clipped, / sound out with her pruned speech."

14. On the other hand, one could argue that the use of *cognominat* instead of *cognominet* was a deliberate change, the indicative producing a bolder, more certain statement.

Performance Practice, *by Antony John*

1. For more information relating to the personnel of Roman choirs in the early baroque, see Noel O'Regan, "The Performance of Roman Sacred Polychoral Music in the Late Sixteenth and Early Seventeenth Centuries: Evidence from Archival Sources," *Performance Practice Review* 8 (1995): 107–46. For a discussion of musical life in Rome during the baroque era, see Silke Leopold, "Rome: Sacred and Secular" in *The Early Baroque Era: From the Late Sixteenth Century to the 1660s*, ed. Curtis Price (Englewood Cliffs, N.J.: Prentice Hall, 1994), 49–74, esp. 54–59.

2. In light of the contemporary preoccupation with polychoral works, it is perhaps not surprising that such platforms were widely used; specific details relating to the size of the platforms and the extent of their use is provided in O'Regan, "Performance of Polychoral Music," 128–35.

3. Tharald Borgir observes that this usage of *basso seguente* is not historically accurate, but is common currency today; see *The Performance of the Basso Continuo in Italian Baroque Music* (Ann Arbor, Mich.: UMI Research Press, 1987), 12–13. For more on the tradition of the *basso seguente*, see Imogene Horsley, "Full and Short Scores in the Accompaniment of Italian Church Music in the Early Baroque," *Journal of the American Musicological Society* 30 (1977): 466–99.

4. For more on the variety of continuo instruments in use in early baroque music, see Paul O'Dette and Jack Ashworth, "Basso Continuo," in *A Performer's Guide to Seventeenth-Century*

Music, ed. Stewart Carter (New York: Schirmer Books, 1997), 269–96, esp. 270–73.

5. Giovanni Piccioni, in the preface to his *Concerti ecclesiastici* of 1610, argues against the use of figures, finding that "to unskilful Organists, they are confusing rather than otherwise, while to the knowledgable and expert, such signs are unnecessary, for they play them correctly by ear and by art." Quoted in Robert Donington, *The Interpretation of Early Music* (New York: W. W. Norton, 1992), 291.

6. Agostini Agazzari, in *Del sonare sopra il basso* (Rome, 1607), explains this idea more fully: "An instrument that serves as foundation must be played with great judgment and due regard for the size of the chorus; if there are many voices one should play with full harmonies, increasing the registers. While if there are few, one should use few consonances, decreasing the registers and playing the work as purely and exactly as possible, using few runs or divisions, occasionally supporting the voices with some contrabass notes and frequently avoiding the high ones which cover up the voices, especially the sopranos or falsettos." Quoted in W. Oliver Strunk, *Source Readings in Music History* (New York: W. W. Norton, 1950), 624.

7. For a discussion of baroque instrumental performance practice, see Howard Mayer Brown and Stanley Sadie, eds., *Performance Practice,* vol. 2, *Music after 1600* (New York: W. W. Norton, 1990). A thorough bibliography of both primary and secondary sources is included on pages 492–511. For a more general introduction to issues relating to the performance of this music, see Mary Cyr, *Performing Baroque Music* (Portland, Oreg.: Amadeus Press, 1992).

8. For more on issues of mensuration, see George Houle, *Meter in Music, 1600–1800: Performance, Perception, and Notation* (Bloomington: Indiana University Press, 1987), 20–29; and Jeffrey Kurtzman, *The Monteverdi Vespers of 1610: Music, Context, Performance* (Oxford: Oxford University Press, 1999), 432–57.

9. Houle proposes a range of MM 60–66 for *tactus maior;* see Houle, ibid., 3–5.

10. See *The New Grove Dictionary of Music and Musicians,* 2d ed., s.v. "Pitch," by Bruce Haynes.

Texts and Translations

Sol

Carolus Troiae columen latinae
imperat Phoebo, velut imperator
Phoebus astrorum face noctilucos
dirigit ignes.

Astra dum caelo secat in rotatus,
astra, caeli militiam sereni,
aetheris scintillivomos Quirites,
nobile vulgus.

Ergo iam senos equitat per orbes
Caroli nomen, superumque caeris
scribitur, qua Mediceis perenne
scribitur astris.

Phoebus hoc caelo canit imperator
Phoebus astrorum nova machinatus,
Carolo quae Principe Medicis co-
gnominat astra.

Saturnus

Io Carole Roma te triumphat,
et te Principe purpurascit ostro,
concolor tibi facta concolori.
Magna Carole Roma te triumphat.
Haec septem dominos sub alta montes
subicit tibi, queis superba tecum
subici tibi gratuletur orbem.
Iusta concipe septicollis urbis
vota Carole, namque frenat omnem
haec urbs unica septicollis orbem.
Tuque Etruria flos virentis orbis,
mera Medicei medulla mellis.

Mercurius

Neque Mercurii lyra delirat,
ubi nubifidas induit alas,
et Mediceis occinit astris.
Huic ergo compescite vestros
compita lusus, pulpita saltus,
tundite motas nablia palmas,
et concordes barbita nervos,
cymbala pulsus, sistra tumultus,
et reboantes tympana flictus,
irrequieti verberis ictus.
Peramabilis audi murmurat ecco,
iam plausu caelum stetit impar.

Texts by Cesare Laurenti (1583–1621)

The Sun

Carlo, glory of Latin Troy,
commands Phoebus, just as Phoebus,
emperor of the stars, directs with his torch
the night-burning fires.

While in the sky he cleaves the stars in his whirling,
the stars, the army of the serene sky,
the sparkling Romans of the airy realm,
the noble populace.

Thus now the name of Carlo gallops
through the six spheres and is written
on the deep-blue pages of the gods,
where it is written forever in the Medicean Stars.

Phoebus sings this to the sky, Phoebus,
emperor of the stars, who has devised new stars
that he names after the Medici,
with Carlo as their prince.

Saturn

Hail, Carlo! Rome celebrates you
and with you as her prince decks herself out in purple,
matching her color to yours.
Great Rome celebrates you, O Carlo!
She has made these seven lordly hills up to their heights
subject to you, on which let her proudly rejoice with you
that the world is subject to you.
Receive, Carlo, the fitting tribute of this seven-hilled city,
for this one seven-hilled city
governs the whole world.
And you, Tuscany, flower of the verdant world,
pure essence of Medicean honey.

Mercury

And nor does Mercury's lyre err
when he puts on his cloud-trusting wings
and sings to the Medicean Stars.
For him, therefore, O tracks, refrain from sport;
O stages, check your dancing;
harps, bruise frenzied hands;
and lutes, strike harmonious strings;
cymbals, pound the beat; sistra, create a din;
and drums, thump resounding blows,
the beat of the restless stick.
Listen, the sweet echo murmurs,
now the sky could not contain the applause.

Translations by Clare Woods

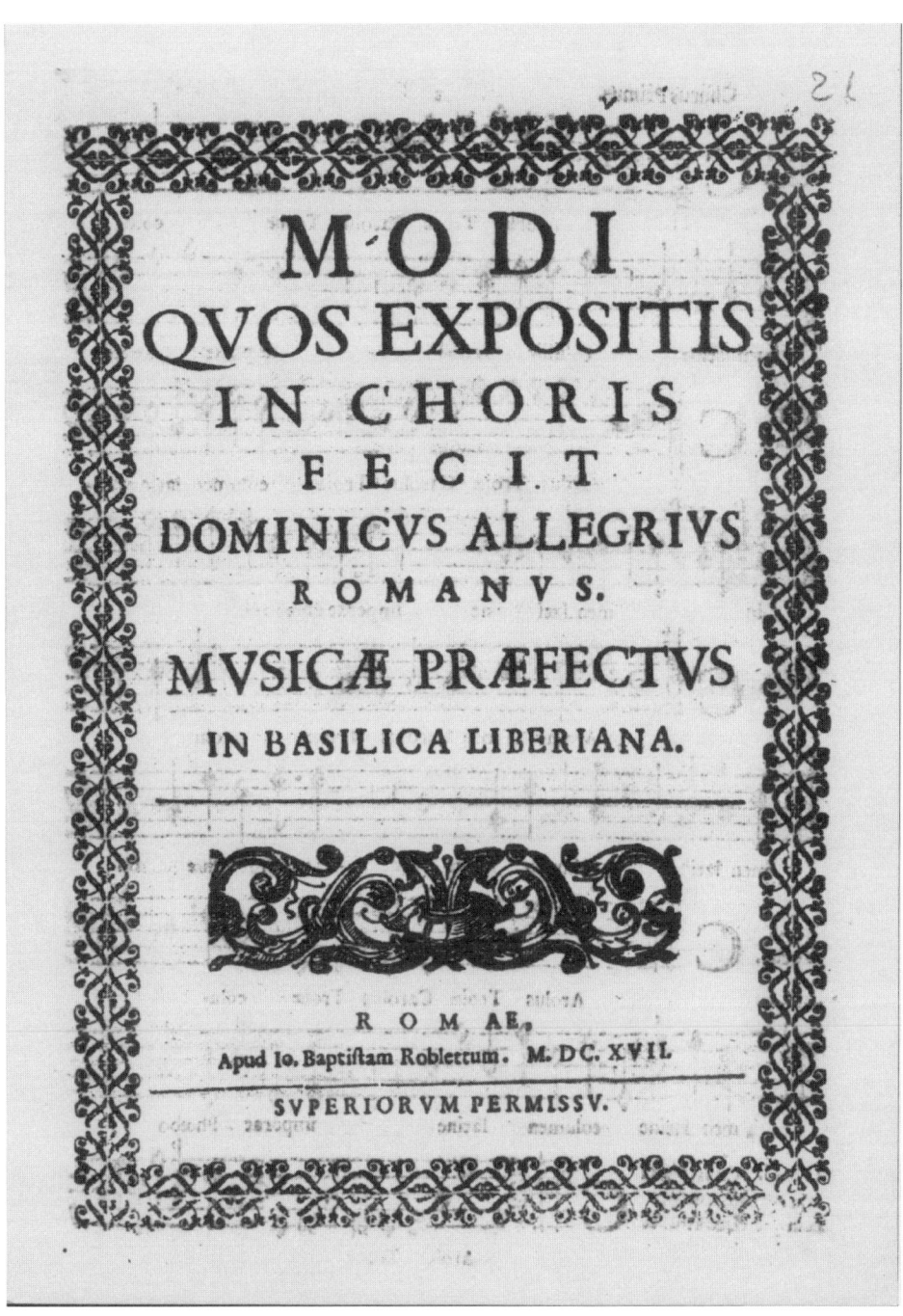

Plate 1. *Modi quos expositis in choris fecit Dominicus Allegrius Romanus Musicae Praefectus in Basilica Liberiana* (Rome, 1617), title page. Courtesy of the Biblioteca Casanatense, Rome.

Plate 2. *Modi quos expositis in choris fecit Dominicus Allegrius Romanus Musicae Praefectus in Basilica Liberiana* (Rome, 1617), page 2, opening measures of "Sol." Courtesy of the Biblioteca Casanatense, Rome.

Plate 3. *Modi quos expositis in choris fecit Dominicus Allegrius Romanus Musicae Praefectus in Basilica Liberiana* (Rome, 1617), page 3, opening measures of "Sol." Courtesy of the Biblioteca Casanatense, Rome.

Music for an Academic Defense

Sol

With the full harmony of voices and instruments

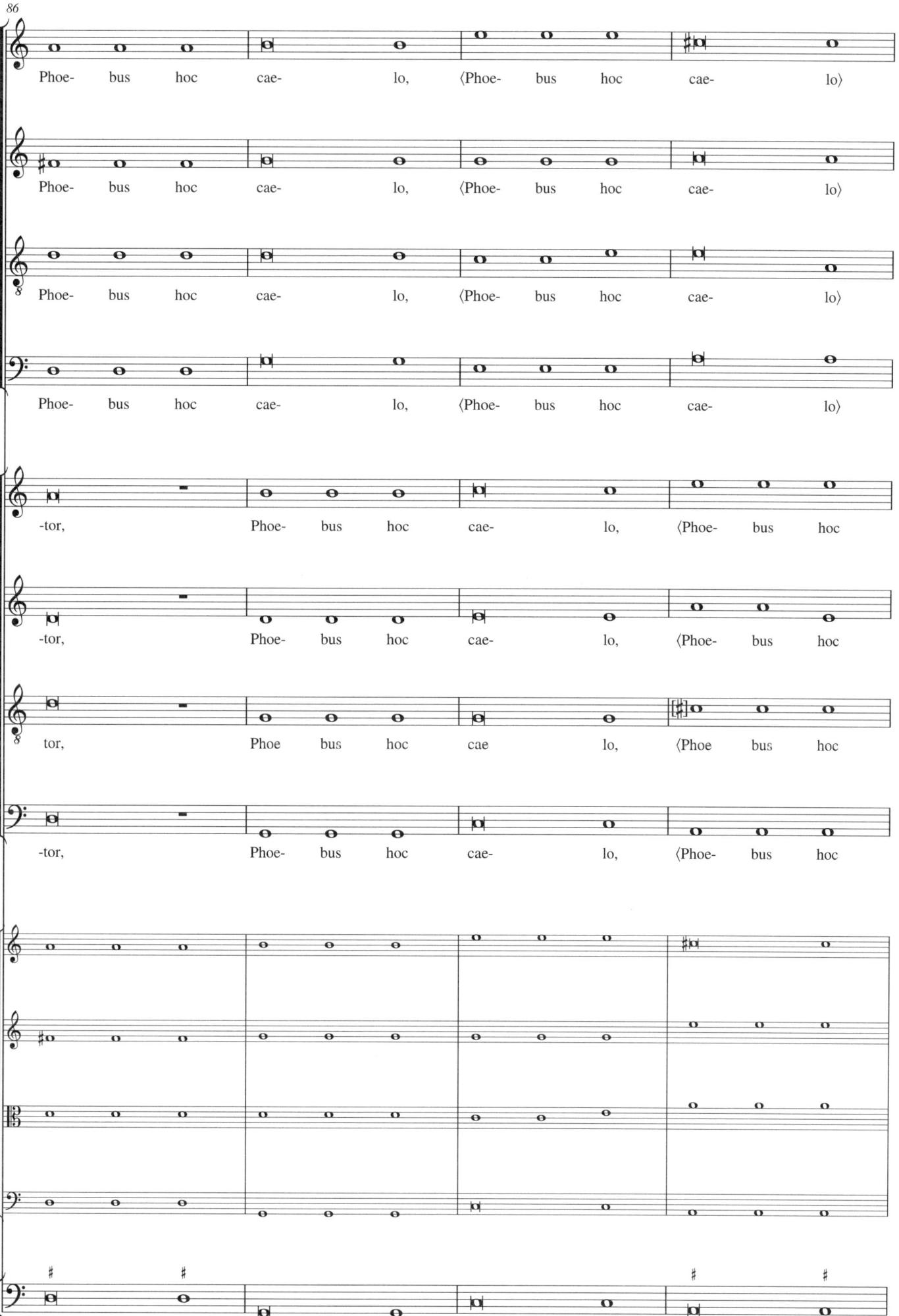

Saturnus

With the full symphony of instruments without winds

Mercurius

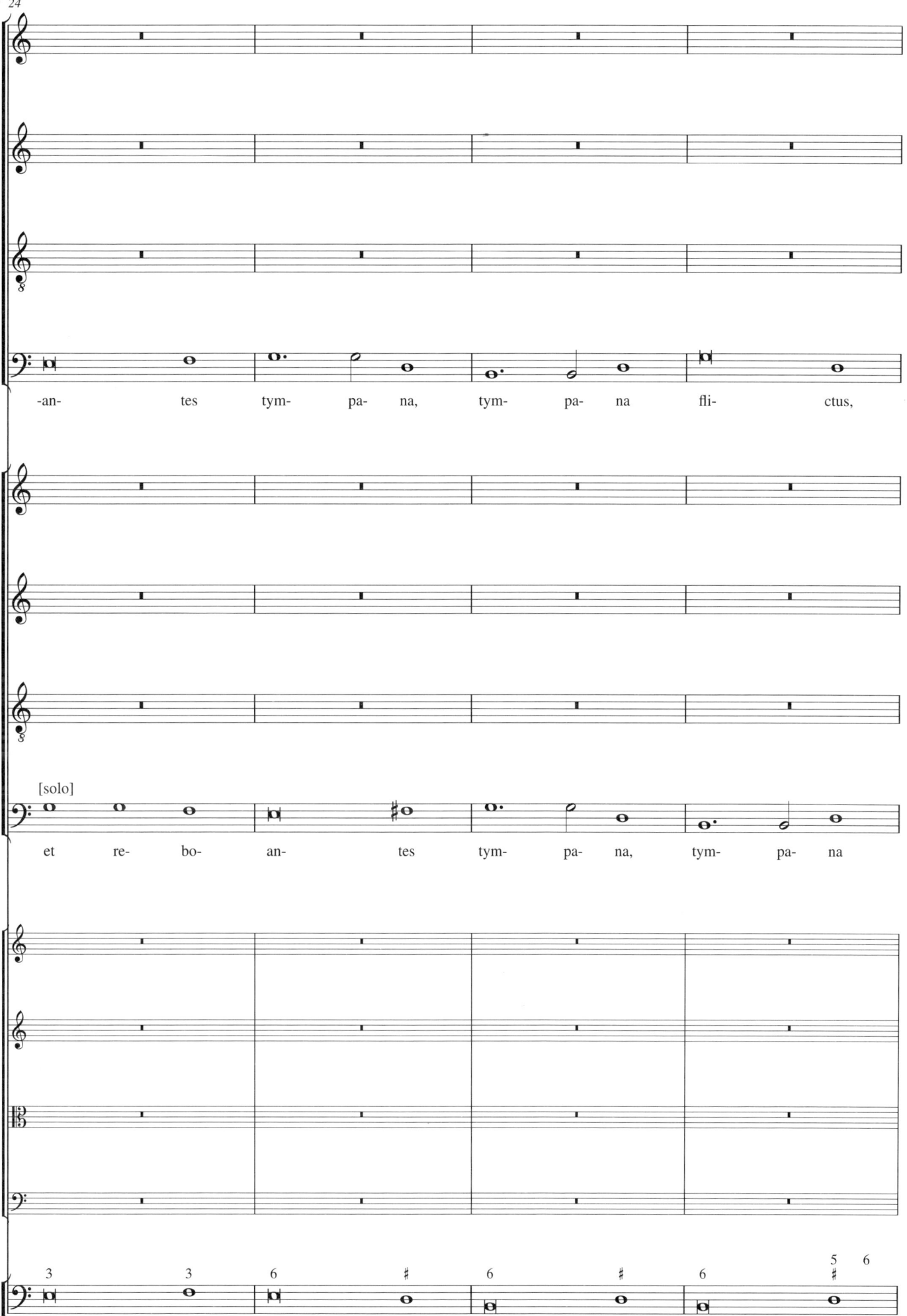

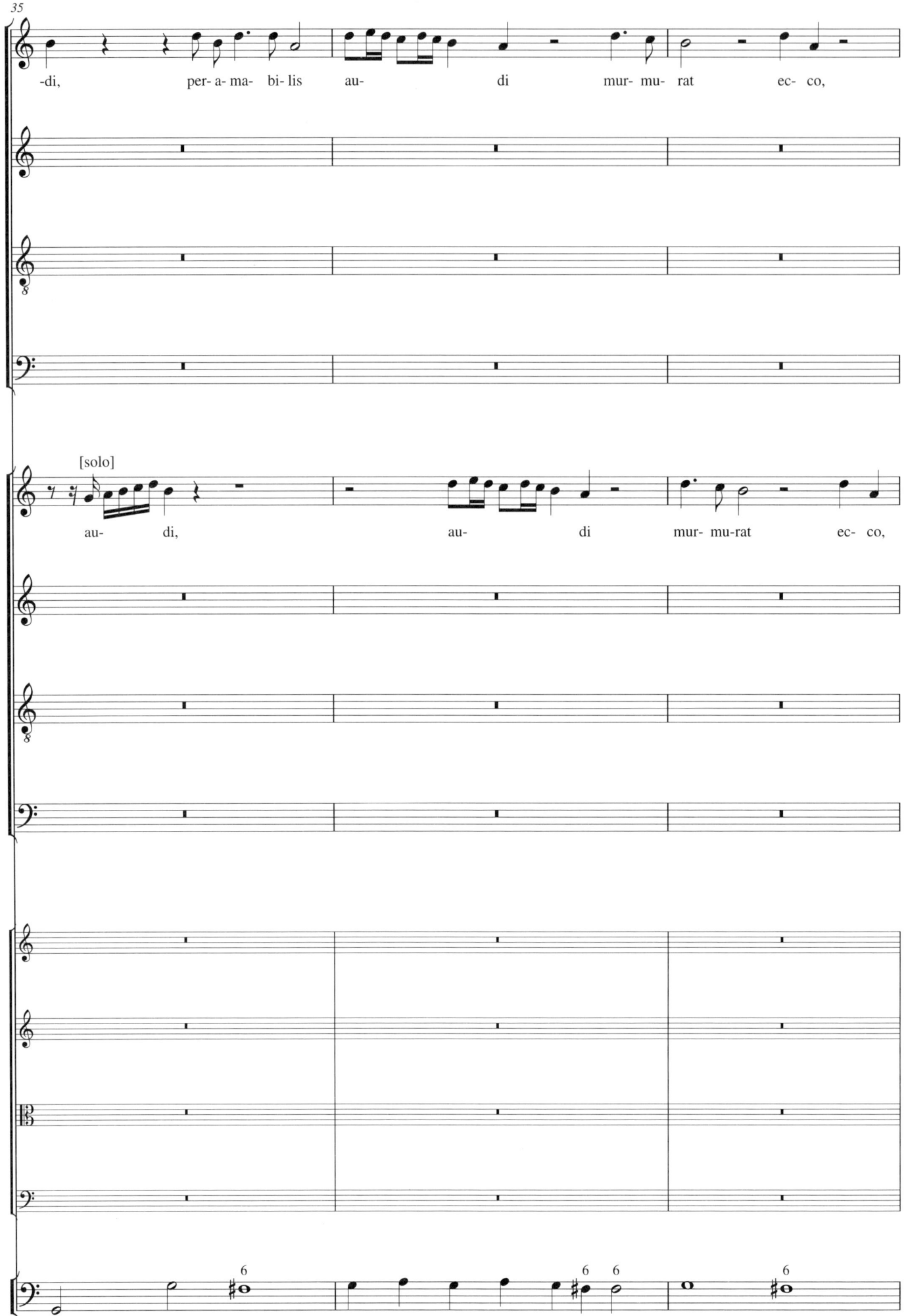

Critical Report

Source

This edition is based on the only surviving source, published by Giovanni Robletti (Rome, 1617):

> MODI | QUOS EXPOSITIS | IN CHORIS | FECIT | DOMINICUS ALLEGRIUS | ROMANUS. | MVSICÆ PRÆFECTUS | IN BASILICA LIBERIANA. | ROMÆ, | Apud Io. Baptistam Roblettum. M. DC. XVII. | SUPERIORUM PERMISSU.

Six extant copies are reported in RISM (A854)[1] in five Italian libraries: Bologna, Civico Museo Bibliografico Musicale; Florence, Conservatorio Statale di Musica Luigi Cherubini; Rome, Biblioteca Casanatense; Rome, Conservatorio di Musica Santa Cecilia (two copies); Rome, Biblioteca Apostolica Vaticana. In fact, RISM would appear to be in error, for despite repeated searching there is no record of the Vatican library source.[2] The score is laid out in choirbook format (see plates 2 and 3), with the parts for the two four-voice choirs, or soloists from the choirs, on facing pages. A bass part for the organ appears with each segment; in one segment (pp. 6–7) separate but identical organ parts are provided for each soloist. In addition to the designation of the voices (Cant., Alt., Ten., Bass., Org.), the parts also carry rubrics that frequently mention instruments, although no additional instrumental parts survive. The layout of the vocal parts suggests that the singers may have performed from this print at the original performance.

Editorial Methods

This edition closely follows the source, except that the parts have been assembled into a score, the text has been underlaid more precisely, a number of notational adjustments have been made for the convenience of modern performers, and several inconsistencies between the parts have been resolved. Modern English equivalents of the original Latin names for the choirs, voice parts, and organ (i.e., Chorus Primus, Chorus Secundus, Cant[us], Alt[us], Ten[or], Bass[us], Org[anum]) are used in the edition. The clefs have been replaced by those to which present-day singers are accustomed. The original clef, mensuration sign, initial rest(s), and first notated pitch in each voice part are shown in an incipit at the beginning of each movement before the brace. The ambitus of each voice part is given after the modern clef and time signature; the main notes show the range of pitches for the choral parts, with any extended ranges required of soloists indicated in parentheses.

Other performance indications, given as rubrics near the part names in the source, have been translated into English and are placed above the staff of the voice part in which they appear in the source (below the staff in the organ); the original Latin forms of the rubrics are given in the critical notes. Editorially added indications are given in brackets. Although no music for accompanying instruments survives, in the present edition string parts have been reconstructed by the editor for performance purposes, following the information conveyed by the Latin rubrics.[3]

The predominant mensuration sign, C, has been rendered as $\frac{4}{2}$, and the sign O3 as $\frac{3}{1}$ (but see the critical notes for "Mercurius," m. 9). Whenever the meter changes within a piece, the original meter and a suggested equivalency formula are given above the staff. Ligatures in the original are marked by a full bracket over the notes. Coloration indicating hemiola in triple meter passages is shown with open horizontal brackets above the notes, while coloration combined with the numeral 3 in duple meters is rendered as a triplet in the edition (e.g., "Mercurius," mm. 6–7, soprano 1 and organ).

The original note values have been retained throughout. The stem directions and rhythmic groupings of notes and rests in the source are made to conform to modern conventions in the edition. Modern vocal beaming has been used throughout. Barlines, absent from the source, have been added as an aid to performers and to help align the parts visually, but they do not imply metrical stress. Notes that continue past a barline in the transcription are divided into appropriate values and connected with a tie. The source indicates double barlines between some sections, and these have been retained in the edition. The final notes preceding double barlines are represented in the source as breves, and these have been preserved in the present edition, resulting in new sections sometimes beginning in the middle of a modern measure (e.g., "Sol," m. 35).

Accidentals on the staff appear in the source and have their normal meanings in modern practice. Accidentals in the source made superfluous by modern barring and convention are eliminated without comment. Editorial and cautionary accidentals have been placed in brackets before the notes to which they apply; unless cancelled they also remain in effect for the remainder of the measure.

Abbreviations in the original text are expanded without comment (for instance, the ampersand is given as "et," while "namq;" is given as "namque"). Archaic conventions of typography, such as the use of *j* for *i* and *v* for *u*, are modernized. The frequent repetitions of words and phrases in the source are set off by commas in the edition. Repetitions of text indicated in the source by *ij* are enclosed in angle brackets.

No figures appear in the original organ part; complete editorial figures have been provided to facilitate performance. Figures have been positioned metrically to correspond to the indicated harmonic changes.

Critical Notes

The following critical notes report all textual and musical differences between the source and the edition that are not otherwise covered in the preceding editorial methods. Locations within each piece are identified by measure number (M., Mm.) and then by voice name. Notes are counted from the beginning of a measure, with each notehead under a tie counted individually; rests are counted separately from notes. The following abbreviations for voice names are employed in the critical notes: S = Soprano, A = Alto, T = Tenor, B = Bass, Org. = Organ, Ch. I = Choir I, Ch. II = Choir II, S1 = Soprano 1, S2 = Soprano 2, etc. The values of notes are given in terms of those in the source and are abbreviated as follows: br = breve (double whole note), sbr = semibreve (whole note), min = minim (half note), smin = semiminim (quarter note), fusa = fusa (eighth note), sfusa = semifusa (sixteenth note). Pitches are identified according to the system in which middle C = c'.

Sol

M. 1, Ch. I, Ch. II, rubric is "Voc. 8"; Org., rubric is "Cum plena vocum instrumentorumque concencione." M. 7, T2, notes 3–4 are smin–smin. M. 11, Org., note 1 is sbr. M. 12, A1, note 1, syllable "-tor" falls under m. 11, note 7. M. 13, S2, note 1, syllable "-tor" falls under m. 12, note 6. M. 14, S2, note 1 is min. M. 17, S2, notes 5–6, text is "lucos." M. 22, T1, rubric is "Duo Ten. Cum totidem fidib."; T2, rubric is "Ten. duo cum totidem fidib."; Org., rubric is "cum duobus Ten." M. 29, S1, rubric is "A 2. Cant. Cum fidib."; S2, rubric is "A 2. Cant."; Org., rubric is "cum duobus Sup." M. 35, Org., rubric is "cum duobus Bas. & plena instrumentorumque simph." M. 45, Ch. I, Ch. II, Org., rubric is "Voc. 8." M. 53, A2, note 1, syllable "-mos" falls under m. 52, note 8. M. 56, T1, Org., rubric is "solum cum fidib." M. 60, T1, note 1, text is "-bis." M. 67, S1, S2, rubric is "cum duobus Sup."; Org., rubric is "cum duobus Cant." M. 68, S2, note 3 is fusa. M. 75, S2, note 2 through m. 76, note 2, syllables "scri-bi-tur a-" fall under m. 75, note 3 to m. 76, note 3. M. 78, Ch. I, rubric is "Voc. 8"; Org., rubric is "cum plena instrum. Symph." M. 82, Ch. 2, rubric is "Voc. 8." M. 101, T2, note 1 through m. 102, note 1, syllable "-tus" and *ij* fall under m. 100, note 2 through m. 101, note 1. Mm. 104–8, Ch. I, and mm. 105–9, Ch. II, text is "Caroloque Principe Medices."

Saturnus

M. 1, Ch. I, Ch. II, rubric is "Voc. 8"; Org., rubric is "cum plena instrum. Symph. s. A." M. 4, Org., note 1 is e (but cf. m. 16, note 1). Mm. 24–29, Ch. II, and mm. 25–29, Ch. I, text is "Consolor tibi facta consolari." M. 28, B1, note 1 is e. M. 31, S1, note 1 is b' (but cf. m. 30, S2, note 1). M. 35, B1, note 2 is sbr; Org., note 2 is sbr. M. 38, B1, rubric is "Voc. 6"; Org., rubric is "Bas. primo cum duob. fidib." M. 38, T1, through m. 45, note 5, clef is on wrong line (C3). M. 43, Org., notes 1–2, pitches unclear. M. 44, Org., note 3 is c. M. 46, Org., notes 1–2 are G–A. M. 49, A2, note 2 is sbr; T2, rest is lacking (or unclear). M. 53, B2, note 4, text is "-ci." M. 59, S1, rubric is "cum Ten."; Org., rubric is "cum Cant. primo, e Ten." M. 62, T1, rubric is "Cant. & Ten." M. 67, T2, rubric is "solus."; Org., rubric is "Ten. solum." M. 69, T2, note 1 text is "-ret-". M. 70, S1, rubric is "A 2. Cant."; S2, rubric is "A 2. Cant. Solus."

Mercurius

M. 1, S1, rubric is "Cum fidib."; Org., rubric is "cum fidib. P. Q." M. 3, S1, note 1, text is "li-". M. 9, Org., rubric is "cum plena instrum. symph."; S2, meter is $\mathbf{O}^3_1$; A2, T2, B2, meter is $\mathbf{C}^3_1$. M. 13, B1, note 6 through m. 14, note 3, text is "conpescita." M. 16, T1, notes 1–5, text is "palpita plausus"; B1, note 1 through m. 17, note 6, text is "rumpite mores"; T2, note 1, text is "-tus." M. 17, S2, note 1 through m. 18, note 1, text is "nobila palma." M. 19, S1, note 1, text is "Cim-"; Org., note 1 is sbr. M. 23, B1, note 2 through m. 26, note 3, text is "roboante timpana." M. 24, B2, note 2 to m. 27, note 3, text is "roboantes timpana." M. 29, Org., rubric is "Omnia instrumenta." M. 34, S1, notes 3–4, tie is original. Mm. 40–41, B1, syllables "-lum ste-tit im-par" fall under m. 39, note 4 through m. 41, note 1. Mm. 42–43, S2, rests are lacking. M. 44, S2, mensuration sign is lacking. M. 45, Ch. I, rest is sbr.

Notes

1. Répertoire International des Sources Musicales, *Einzeldrucke vor 1800*, ser. A/I, 9 vols. (Kassel: Bärenreiter, 1971–81), s.v. "A854."

2. Thanks to Michael Dodds for bringing this fact to my attention.

3. In his entry on Allegri in *Dizionario biografico degli Italiani* (Rome: Società Grafica Romana, 1960), Alberto Pironti seems to imply the existence of separate instrumental parts in Allegri's *Modi*: "As a composer, Allegri was one of the first authors to provide independent instrumental accompaniment to the singing, writing for the instruments parts which served to introduce the singing, to give the singers a rest, [and to strengthen] the final cadence" (Come compositore, l'A. è uno dei primi autori che diedero al canto un accompagnamento strumentale non all'unisono, scrivendo per gli strumenti parti che servissero di introduzione al canto, di riposo ai cantori nel mezzo, di clausola alla fine). It may be, however, that he drew his conclusions from the Latin rubrics.

The rubrics may be the root of another commonly identified feature of the work, attributable to Thurston Dart's entry on Allegri in *Grove's Dictionary of Music and Musicians*, 5th ed. (1954): "In his 'Modi quos expositis in choris' (Rome, 1617) he included some solos and duets with accompaniments for violins. These instruments are muted in the solos—one of the earliest examples of mutes for string instruments." In fact, the only implication that mutes were to be used comes at the beginning of "Mercurius," where the organ part carries the rubric "cum fidib. P. Q." The abbreviation "P. Q." may stand for "per quietes" (lit., quietly). Thanks to Pamela Whitcomb for providing the solution to this issue.